RUNNING the RED LINE

What Readers Say:

Inspirational. I read this book and it's truly motivating. So well written and easy to read. (**J. Norton**)

It's one of those books that is hugely readable and which also offers, for those who want to pause and reflect, an opportunity to learn something really, really useful. (**Wendy Robinson**)

Excellent book, I couldn't put it down. The author gives an incredibly honest account of her life as a runner, climber and as a human. Really great book. (**Ricky Parrish**)

This is a brilliant book, very inspiring and well worth reading. You don't need to be a fell runner to enjoy the journey. What an inspiration to get out and find what you truly love. (**Cathy Woodhead**)

It's difficult not to use too many superlatives in describing this book, it stacks up alongside the best that has been written on the subject and deserves recognition and applause. Perhaps the highest praise I can give is to say that I wish I could have written it. A++ (**Alpine Trekker**)

This book inspired me to be a proper fell runner. It made me realise we all have so much more in us, if only we just put our minds to it. (**Amazon Reviewer**)

Julie Carter though has perfected the art of balancing the factual matters with the personal and emotional side. It's no mean feat but ensured, for me at least, that I was totally absorbed in the book from start to finish. Having enjoyed this book so much, I recommended it to friends and they seem to have enjoyed it as much as I did. (**Amazon Reviewer**)

I read over a few days because I couldn't put it down. An inspirational and motivating insight (**LD Winter**)

I thoroughly enjoyed reading Running The Red Line, it made me laugh and cry but most of all it inspired me to get out there and run. Julie's humorous, self-effacing, honest style makes Running the Red Line outstanding in it's genre. (**Wyn Clayton**)

A book I am now reading for the second time. Julie has inspired me to listen and train the thoughts going on in my head into a power which supersedes the aches in my legs!!! Read it, you will not be disappointed. **(Amazon Reviewer)**

There is an excellent marriage of technical and emotional detail with not an overdose of either. I heartily recommend this book to all runners and to anyone else who suspects their hobby is also their passion. **(Amazon Reviewer)**

A most enjoyable read by a remarkable woman. Makes you want to get up and go for a run on the fells. **(Ken Owens)**

I thought this was a wonderful book, and would really recommend it to anyone. Brilliantly told, thought-provoking and absorbing. I couldn't put it down. **(Rachel Mellor)**

This is a special book. It's honest, interesting, often funny and a brave account. I felt compelled to keep reading at the end of each chapter to find out more. I thoroughly recommend it. **(Lorraine Jackson)**

A fantastic book, written with passion, thoughtfulness and brutal honesty. The life experiences are as equally fascinating as the physical endeavours. **(Dr E Gamble)**

Love the great breadth of philosophy, wisdom, medicine and running from this incredible woman. Action-packed, and vastly entertaining! **(Angela J Lock)**

From first fell race to British champion, the worst life can throw at you to the best. Julie's book is moving & inspiring. Resilience is often talked about but never better illustrated, read it. **(Lindsay Buck)**

An amazing read! Even though I'm definitely not a runner I could relate to Julie's personal story. Her insights and little gems of wisdom will stay with me. **(Amazon Reviewer)**

An inspiring book. Makes you laugh and cry. A great read. **(Sam Ayers)**

Excellently written, totally awe inspiring and uplifting. Thoroughly recommended whether you are into running or not. **(Jill Kingdon)**

RUNNING
the RED
LINE

Julie Carter

MindFell

Published in 2023 by Mindfell

Copyright © 2023 Julie Carter

First published 2018

Third edition 2023

Julie Carter has asserted her right to be identified as the author of this Work in accordance with the Copyright, Designs and Patents Act 1988

ISBN: 978-1-9999554-4-1

A CIP catalogue copy of this book can be found in the British Library.

Published with the help of Indie Authors World
www.indieauthorsworld.com

IndieAuthors
World

This book is dedicated to Kit Stewart

1947-2005

Contents

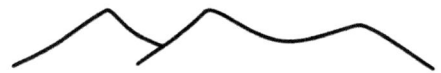

A Journey into the Mind of Mountain Running

She's running near the red line

knocking on Heaven's door.

She's been this way so often

but not raced this fell before

She's running near the red line

burning fire from within.

It's not just slaying dragons

or confessing all her sins

She's running on the red line

holding on for all she's worth

Every second counts now

Cos we're not long on this earth

She's pushing back the red line,

muddy, sweaty and uncouth.

Racing to her limit.

Seeking out the truth.

Julie Carter

Preface to the Second Edition

Some dictionary definitions of a Red Line:

- *A boundary or limit which cannot be crossed.*

- *The maximum revolutions per minute of an engine.*

- *A marker beyond which a person is unwilling to negotiate.*

- *A limit past which safety can no longer be guaranteed.*

Since publishing the first edition of this book I have had a steady stream of encounters, both in person and online, in which people from various walks of life have told me about their own red lines and how they have shifted these boundaries in order to live a bigger and richer life. I'm not necessarily talking about winning medals or setting records. I am talking about having personal experiences which bring a depth of happiness and fulfilment one might not have thought possible. I would like to thank all the people who have been in touch with me and talked about what my book has meant to them. You have in turn spurred me on to improve the book in various ways, and to carry on writing and publishing new work.

It is my belief that books can help us to learn but they cannot deliver learning to us in a package. We must manufacture our own package. Books can open our eyes and our minds, give us different ideas and perspectives and through sparking our imagination they can awaken new feelings and possibilities. But to really know something we must experience it first-hand. As I once wrote about the experience of running in a lightning storm, "You cannot put the taste of electricity on a postcard".

This is not a self-help book; I would not appoint myself in such a lofty role. *Running the Red Line* is a story. I do include reflections and weave in some science, psychology, and philosophy to make the story more useful and to clarify its meaning. People tell me it is a book that has helped them with their own meanings and spurred them on in their own experiences. Sharing our stories in this way is an essential ingredient of our humanity. One of the best parts of being a writer is making connections with people and I hope one of those people is you. I hope you enjoy the book and please feel free to get in touch with me.

Best wishes

Julie Carter

One

In the Flow

Suddenly, I found the on switch, the other gear, and it was like entering a different world. Like a character in a C S Lewis's story, I had gone through the back of the wardrobe and was now in the realm of fantasy. Feet barely touching the ground, the spring of the grassy fell on each fleeting touch down, unhurriedly fast. I became aware of how to land so lightly it was hardly a landing at all before I was back in the air. With a heightened awareness of each tussock and mud patch, choosing the best grassy line. Leaning into the descent without resisting. Shafts of sunlight streaming over the fields far below. I was flying through the warm summer's evening. These hills had been my solace for nigh on thirty years, but this was a new kind of magic. The depths of my lungs opened up as if taking in a shock. Thrilled, amazed, awakened. What spell had transformed me and swept me away? On and on I flew down the fellside. No, I was not dreaming: this was real; this was my first proper fell race.

There are certain moments in a person's life that are unforgettable: the birth of our children, the death of someone we love, falling in love, getting married, Sunderland winning the FA cup. Special, powerful moments are etched into us. Recollection of normal days and routine events is often shaky and sketchy as if our brains do not put that much effort into storing unimportant details. But when something important happens, it feels as if the whole process of creating a memory is different. Certain highly meaningful experiences become part of our very fabric. This memory of an evening fell race in the early summer of 2004 has this truly indelible quality. This recollection is so vivid and feels so unforgettable that it must have registered in my mind as a very special experience.

I have had many special experiences through fell running, and the purpose of this book is not simply to share some of these but also to reflect on, and share, their meaning. This is a book about feelings and thoughts, about mind and body and about how sport, or any creative activity which is fully engaged with, can enrich and strengthen a life. The way we approach our sport and our lives has a large bearing on what we get back, both in terms of our performance and our satisfaction. All good stories contain meaning, and, even though some of the meanings in my own stories appear to contradict each other at times, I will try to make sense of them, calling on the knowledge of experts in science, psychology and sport to help me.

There is only one true expert in any of our lives, but, in sharing our stories, reflections and insights, we can sometimes help each other's quest to live a fulfilled life. We all have our red lines, which represent our real limits, but we tend to live with a large margin between what we do and what we can do. There are times in life when we want and need that margin, and there are times when we don't. I have found most rewards when choosing to get nearer to my heart's desires and live out my potential, and, in this endeavour, fell running has been one of my most effective teachers.

That first fell race at Blencathra was only a few weeks after I had moved to Cumbria with my partner, Mandy, and our dog, Holly the foxhound, and started working as a GP. We had bought a very ramshackle farmhouse in Ennerdale, where it would be two years before anything better than cardboard would grace the living room floor. For a while, I had been having an idea that I wanted to do a fell race. At university over twenty years earlier, I had competed in cross-country races and, since then, had kept up a bit of very casual running to keep fit for climbing. I cannot remember exactly how or why this impulse to run a fell race came about. At the time, I did not know, or mix with, any fell runners, and really, when I look back, I knew hardly anything about the sport. I had bought some special fell running shoes, though, and had been out practising for a few weeks, taking delight in the amazing opportunity to go for a run on the fells from my own front door after a day at work.

On that sunny evening in June, I don't remember feeling nervous or worried about entering the Blencathra Fell Race. It was a friendly affair: you just needed to turn up and pay a pound or two to the chap giving out race numbers from the boot of his car. I do remember it was hard work up to the summit but tried to keep up with the main bunch of the field of runners, as I did not really know where I was going. Also, I was a bit unsure of how to approach racing up a mountain but was glad when I realised that it seemed to be the done thing amongst the competitors around me to use a walking stride up the steeper sections. The view from the summit over to Derwentwater was wonderful, although there was not much time to take it in before haring off down the mountain. The race returns to Mungrisdale over the grassy Souther Fell, famed for its resident *spectral army* of ghosts in the form of a legion on the march. When I was running down Souther Fell, something began to work. My legs were going as fast as possible, feet hardly touching the ground, and I began to feel as if I was flying. I was swallowed up into a feeling of complete freedom. I can even remember the green colour of the grass as if I had never seen green before. I was only just in control and felt on the threshold of recklessness. I was at once both abandoned and fully engaged. Lost and found. During these moments, a thought rang through my head: *I love this!!*

The fell bottomed out into lumpy tussocks over fields, giving way to a short rough track to the finish. It was not the last time I would arrive, at the end of a race, back where I had started, but feeling as if I was in a different world with a different take on life. At the age of thirteen my life was revolutionised by a school residential in Borrowdale and since then I had regularly sought inspiration, strength and comfort in the Cumbrian fells. In my early twenties, I took up rock climbing, and, at times when leading a climb on an exposed crag, I came to know this feeling of total and complete concentration and engagement. However, I did not know there was another, an altogether different, way of feeling that kind of wild pleasure by running on the fells.

In that run down Souther Fell, I was in a state of *flow*. Flow is the Holy Grail of sport, and I found it on my first proper fell race. But, on subsequent races, I was to discover that flow can prove to be very elusive indeed. In fact, it would take some years before I realised that it is possible to actively nurture the conditions encouraging flow to occur. For a long time, I assumed it was a matter of luck, and, from time to time, I did get lucky and fall into a state of flow. Those moments are etched into me just like the Blencathra race. But it is only relatively recently that I have come to know how it is that achieving flow is not simply down to luck.

Flow can also be described as being *in the zone*. Although, to me, that phrase implies a narrowing of focus, as in people playing video games, unable to be distracted and completely zoned out, not connected to the world. I like to think that, when you are in flow, you are as fully connected as possible and all the senses are heightened – not diminished. In sports psychology, flow is defined as: "The mental state of operation in which a person performing an activity is fully immersed in a feeling of energised focus, full involvement in, and enjoyment of, the process of the activity. In essence, flow is characterised by complete absorption in what one does." Is that not tantalising?

The Hungarian psychologist Mihaly Csikszentmihalyi pioneered the concept of flow, and he describes it as the "psychology of engagement". As a teenager on holiday, Csikszentmihalyi had no money for the cinema so, instead, went to a free talk by someone he had never heard of, Carl Jung, and this talk inspired him to study psychology and make it his life's work. Mihaly had been a child refugee from the Second World War but noticed, as he was growing up in the post-war era, that a lot of the adult refugees seemed to remain very troubled and unfulfilled, as if they could not make peace with themselves and were unable to feel secure in their new lives. These observations motivated him to undertake a serious exploration to identify the ingredients which make a life worth living. Initially, he researched poets and musicians but then moved on to include athletes, looking at the way they became totally creatively engaged. He found that the defining thing they had in common was the happiness they gained from this state of immersion which he termed "flow".

In sports psychology nowadays, athletes are encouraged to achieve the state of flow as a method of gaining competitive advantage. When you are in flow, you maximise the chances of performing at your best. I am sure this is true, but there is a paradox here because you cannot really flow while directly focusing on the final goal. Flow is a moment-by-moment experience where what is happening now is so completely absorbing that what will happen next is not on your mind. Notice that the definition says, "...full involvement in, and enjoyment of, the *process* of the activity".

When it comes to fell racing, pacing is important, and you cannot simply rely on running according to your moment-by-moment feelings. Tactics come into play, and sometimes you need to hold back and run at a pace which can seem too comfortable to be fully flowing. In an extremely long race in particular, it is important to learn how to measure the effort. It is all too common for a runner to go out too fast and fight to keep up the pace, only to find they slow down terribly and struggle to carry on. I have found that the best way to judge pace is if I am only just able to overtake others or to fend off a challenge at the end – then I have paced myself well. And I do mean *only just*. After a few races like that my body started to understand and remember what a sustainable race pace feels like. During the time when I am holding back a bit, there can be a tendency to let my mind get involved in worries, and I've learnt that worrying will inhibit flow. I think, however, that, with practice, a runner can learn to flow regardless of whether they are working hard or taking it easy. Flow will not come in every race, and I have never been in flow for an entire race. That may be because I have not paid enough attention to achieving this state and instead focused on other things, such as worrying about where my rivals are or just being worried about not doing well enough. One thing I realise now is that flow can never happen if you are tense.

This is a major part of the flow paradox. If you are trying too hard, it does not happen. I was recently trying a climb on the indoor climbing wall, which I had really struggled to do quite a few times because it was so strenuous. I could almost do it, but, every time, I had to stop and rest just before getting to the top.

One day, I tried not focusing on the climbing but instead thought about my breathing and, as a result, got up the wall easily and was relaxed without feeling tired at all. Over the years, I have realised how much energy I waste on trying too hard at just about everything I do. Some sages may describe this as a symptom of being too anxious about outcomes. At the moment, I am learning to swim, and it's really interesting. When I slow down, relax and concentrate more on my stroke rather than gritting my teeth, tensing up and pushing on to get through the lengths, then swimming begins to happen. Well, something vaguely approximating to swimming! I am trying to be relaxed and to avoid living up to my swimming teacher's description of me, "Like a boxer at the start of a fight!"

Another interesting thing about flow is its relationship to desire: wanting to do well, wanting a personal best or wanting to win. If I did not care about those things, why not just run a tiny bit more slowly and make it relatively comfortable? Competing to your limit can hurt at times, and, for most people, racing hard involves some pain. A few months ago, I went to a talk by the famous Borrowdale fell runner Billy Bland. Many of Billy's records were set over thirty years ago, and hardly anyone has come close to his achievements since. So impressive were his feats that he is widely and respectfully referred to as *King Billy*. When asked about how he coped with pain, he said he never felt any. Perhaps, at some level, he did feel pain, or perhaps his brain was otherwise occupied, focused totally on the step-by-step, breath-by-breath act of running. When you see a film of Billy running down a fell, it certainly is a vision of flow. He almost looks as if he's defying the laws of physics and flying. He definitely looks as if he's enjoying himself!

Could it be true that Billy was just so good he could cruise around comfortably without the pain of full effort, not really caring, and still beat everyone else? Is it more effective not to care about performance, not to have competitive desires so that you can feel relaxed? Well, it might be okay if you are not truly competitive, but it's not the way to run your fastest or, in my experience, to feel your best. You do need desire. You do need energy. You do need to know where the power dial is and how to turn it up. So my guess is that, while actually trying hard, Billy was a master of channelling his energy. The ability to channel energy depends on another crucial ingredient: focus. Focus not on the outcome but on the second-by-second execution. Without concentration on channelling the inner drive, the burning fire of desire to run well, the focus can be lost and the brain can look for something else to attend to: sometimes pain or something much worse, fear.

When you get to a race and your thoughts are directly focused on the desired outcome, then the inevitable will happen. You will start to feel fear. The fear of failure. The fear of failure is something almost all of us who have experienced a conventional school education have learnt. Many of us have learnt this lesson far too well. It's hard to unlearn things and replace those ingrained, almost reflexive, thoughts with a different way of thinking. It involves creating new pathways in the brain and making those pathways familiar. The common analogy is that of blazing a trail through snow. Once the track is made, it is much easier to follow, but, without use, the path will get blown over after it snows again. Which why it is a bad idea to keep practicing the things which do not help us. At the start of a race, I do not forget about wanting to do well, but I think the trick is to try to hold onto that wanting as a visceral, bodily feeling, the fire in the belly, as if there is an engine inside of me waiting to respond to stepping on the gas. But actual thoughts? I am beginning to realise that it is very important not only what we think about but also that we can choose what to think. With practice, it gets easier to direct the thinking brain. In my work as a GP, I have met countless people with various mental-health problems who are stuck with unhelpful, sometimes consuming and obsessive, thoughts and worries. I try to teach them how they can think differently; when we are calm we can choose how to focus our thinking brain; we have that free will. We can blaze new trails in the snow. It sounds so easy, but, like a lot of things, taking control of our own thoughts demands patience and practice. So racing is the perfect opportunity for me to try to take a dose of my own medicine. At times I have found it impossibly hard not to be hijacked by my own thoughts and maybe that has given me an insight into why other people might find it hard too.

Before and during a race, I no longer allow myself to worry about the outcome I want; that feels horrible. Instead, I try to think about much simpler things: shoes, shoe laces, safety pins, bum bag, the sky, the grass, relaxing my posture, breathing, smiling. Thinking about simple concrete things cannot generate a worry. To do this, you have to have done all the thinking well beforehand: the route, the clothes, the food all these need to be sorted out before you leave home. That way it's okay to instruct the mind not to worry; it can relax knowing that everything is taken care of. If the impulse to worry gains a hold, then I apply the *Keswick Womens' flapping theory*, which I have learnt from my team-mates. In an effort to divert the worrying brain, the theory directs one to engage in low-key activities, such as putting on and taking off three or four different items of clothing several times each, going for a wee with a totally empty bladder or checking the contents of the bum bag, again. These types of pre-race behaviours can all act as successful decoys preventing the brain from becoming overly focused on fears of failure and pain. Of course, it's better not to need to resort to these diversions and learn to be calm and in control, but, once the race starts, then it's only about breathing, pacing, releasing unhelpful tension and focusing on the job in hand, running, just running. I guess that's what I aspire to because when, on the odd occasion, I actually manage it, the feeling is wonderful!

The Blencathra Fell Race was not the first time I felt the flow of running. I had started running as an undergraduate student and enjoyed competing as a member of the university cross-country team. Recently, I was surprised to discover a poem I had written when I was in my early twenties. I remember writing the poem about one particular run, a very modest and sedately paced run, around the hills above Bath, where I was working at the time. I guess the reason I felt the flow of running then was that I was recovering from being seriously ill with typhoid and was weak for months afterwards until one day my running legs started to come back.

After I had graduated in Biology and Genetics, I worked in a lab for a while before travelling to India and Nepal on my own. I flew from Heathrow to Delhi, the first time I had ever been on an airplane. I had a rich and wonderful few months trekking in the high mountains and ending with two weeks in a Buddhist monastery. But, as I flew home, I was unaware that I was incubating more than ideas. A few hours after getting back to the UK, I was struck down with a fever and was discovered unconscious in my flat that night. When I was in hospital with typhoid, I suffered some complications and, at times, thought I might be dying. Later, I realised there had been times when those fears had been shared by my friends as well as doctors. So to be able to be up and out and running again was an unbelievable freedom, and this is what it felt like:

Running

Beating fast, steady strides

drawing from the well of life,

all I feel is all that's there:

golden sunlight, stinging air.

Breathing in all I can

running now, but never ran.

Never past, never seen

never future, never dream.

In each moment all is me.

The flow

of pure

Energy

In fact, owing to the effects of the illness I struggled with any regular hard exercise for years and took up rock climbing because, at my level, it was less physically demanding. I ran occasionally during the rest of my twenties and throughout my thirties but was sure that doing a race of any kind was a thing of the past. It was not until after I was forty and came to live in Cumbria that running became important to me. I would still be hard pushed to say which sport I love more, but I guess they both involve a lot of the same things, the foremost among them being the opportunity to find the edge of my comfort zone on the fells and mountains. After all, as my wise friend Nicky Forbes likes to remind me, "Life begins at the edge of one's comfort zone."

My next notable memory of fell running certainly did not involve much comfort. I turned up at my second proper fell race as green as the grass on Souther Fell. It was a foul, foul day in

Seathwaite as I set off on my first Duddon. One of the famous six Lakeland Classic races, the Duddon, is over eighteen miles with six thousand feet of ascent.

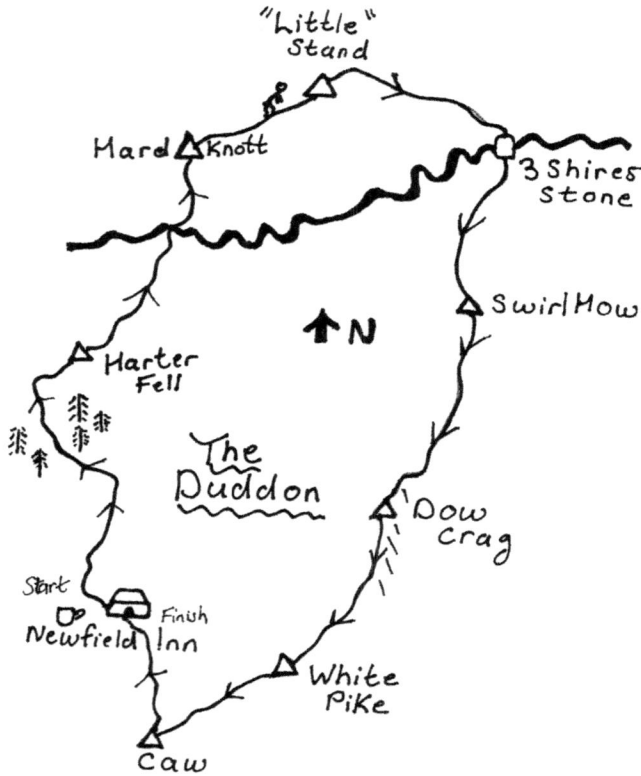

The summits of Harter Fell and Hardknott were hard going in the howling wind and lashing rain, but the paths were not difficult to follow, and there were plenty of fellow runners to plod along with at this stage. Then awaiting us was the ascent of Little Stand, a notorious joke among fell runners on account of it being at least as high as Everest and probably steeper. I was shocked at the sheer effort required but then realised I would need more than physical effort to get through this. A smattering of route preparation would have certainly come in handy. After Little Stand was behind me, my troubles had only just begun.

Brought to a halt by not knowing which direction to run in and, by now alone in the mist, I was wrestling with the map like a sail in the wind and grappling to get a compass bearing. It was not quite what I had bargained for. By some fluke of luck, as I pressed on navigating through the mirk, I arrived at the Three Shires Stone checkpoint and continued on up Swirl How and Dow Crag. I simply could not believe how hard and long this race was and how it went on and on and on. Although I had full *waterproofs* on, every fibre of my clothing was saturated as I was coming off the summit of Dow. I needed a wee but was not physically capable of pulling down my pants, so I wee'd in them. Still, I thought that nobody would know and that it couldn't be that much further until I reached the end. I began to fear that I might be last and that everyone else would have gone home by now, but then a chirpy couple coming off White Pike caught up with me. The chap made a friendly, casual remark about just one more hill. *What!! Another hill.* I was horrified and had no idea we had another fell to do.

"Yes, there's Caw to do yet."

No – it just could not be possible. Soaked and exhausted, we plodded diligently onwards, through bog and mist, when two figures, running directly towards us in the opposite direction, appeared and enquired:

"Have you been to Caw?"

"No. Have you?"

"No."

"Oh."

In hopeful desperation the bunch of us set off on a different bearing to find the summit. At the top, we fumbled under our jackets with frozen hands to punch the orienteering stamp on our race numbers as proof we had made it to the checkpoint. I soon lost the group in the mist but managed to get back to the finish in one piece, arriving at Seathwaite in well over six hours. I felt I had been lucky, but differently lucky. I was not prepared for what I had just been through and only just managed to get away with it. It had been a bit sobering. Driving home, heater on full pelt, I pondered. This fell racing is a seriously hard thing. I wondered if it was for real people or superhumans, made of stronger stuff than me. I was not sure what to think. I was cold, exhausted and hungry and sensed I had an awful lot to learn.

Two

The Limits to What You Can Achieve

Defining moments are moments when possibility becomes inevitability. They can sometimes seem rather random and can occasionally have a slightly spooky, predestined feeling. Something happens to give one a nudge or a prompt. Events start moving in a certain direction, and momentum builds.

All the cells in our body start life with the possibility to become anything: a nose cell, a liver cell, a nerve. But crucial things are switched on and off in order to make the cells go down their own paths, and, once those genetic switches have been pulled, there is no going back. Past a certain point, the cells are committed to their destinies. It was like this for me when my Bob Graham Round switch got pulled. Something inside me was switched on, and my destiny became defined. This is how it happened.

The Bob Graham Round is an iconic challenge, the first real ultra-running route in the British mountains. In 1932, at the age of forty-two, Bob Graham ran his round in twenty-three hours and thirty-nine minutes, covering forty-two Lakeland summits and a questionable number of miles, somewhere between sixty-six and seventy. It took twenty-eight years for the round to be repeated in under twenty-four hours, although nearly two thousand devotees of the fells have managed it now. Most people who like long-distance fell running entertain thoughts of *doing the Bob* at some point. Some racing snakes decide against it because it is said that running that kind of distance ruins your speed. Just as well then that, as I had only just begun fell running, I had no speed to ruin.

In 2005, six friends set off on an alpine climbing holiday in Chamonix. It was a few days after the London bombings, often referred to as 7/7, and, as we made for the airport, there was a mood of shock and sadness because we were not yet accustomed to living in the age of terror. I was keen to be distracted by my holiday read, *Feet in the Clouds* by Keswick Athletics Club runner Richard Askwith. The Bob Graham Round features strongly in Richard's wonderful book, in which he goes into a lot of fell running history. During the holiday, my partner, Mandy, and her close friend Kit were doing some long rock climbs while the other four of us were donning our big boots and crampons and going mountaineering. On a serene and cloudless morning, we made a pre-dawn start to enjoy a very satisfying ascent of the beautiful icy pyramid of the Aiguille d'Argentière. The climb involves an unrelentingly steep snow slope, and, as the air thins, the going gets harder. I was roped up to my friend Martha, who began to struggle a little with the altitude but lacked nothing in the determination department. Every few minutes, she would stop for essential oxygen replenishment, slumping over her ice axe yet looking resolutely up the slope. She would then utter the words "right then", by which I could tell she meant she would keep going until the top, only to be forced to have another rest minutes later. Martha, as always, expected a lot of herself, and we made excellent time to the 3,901-metre summit. After a picnic and photos, we made our way down and, by the middle of the day, were descending the long and tiring Argentière glacier and the four of us had joined together on one rope. When the sun gets on a glacier in the afternoon, it can be like marching through a desert, and, by this time, I was feeling sapped of all energy, dried out and baked as we traipsed across soft snow in blazing heat. On a crevassed glacier, you have to concentrate and walk in the same line and at the same pace as your companions, not pulling on the rope but not letting slack develop either in case one of the party does go through the snow into a yawning hole underneath. There we were, plodding on, the four of us, John, Pete, Martha and I, one after the other silently absorbed in our own thoughts, until we took a welcome break amongst some rocks and I began chatting to Pete. A long-standing friend and an accomplished orienteer, Pete had lured me into a couple of off-road races when I was a biology student in York. He was working at the university, a real athlete and scientist. I always looked up to Pete and took his advice seriously. In fact, it was probably Pete's influence all those years earlier that had sparked off my interest in fell running in the first place.

"Pete."

"Yes."

I hesitated.

"Yes, what?"

"Do you think there is any chance I could do the Bob Graham Round?"

Pete was so good, kind, thoughtful and encouraging, hugely supportive and such a great friend. I was thus totally taken aback by his reply.

"I think you'll find, Julie, that there is a limit to what you can achieve."

We got back on the glacier and again trudged on in silence. I was flabbergasted, wounded, hurt. To this day, I do not know if he did it on purpose. Was he goading me to get serious about fell running? I can see that it was an improbable thing for me to ask, since I had hardly any real fell running experience – definitely much less than most people who attempt the round. I might not have known much about fell running but I knew enough about myself to recognise when a gauntlet had emphatically been thrown down. By the time we got back to the campsite and had the kettle on, my mind was made up. I was going to attempt the Bob Graham Round.

During the next few days, Martha, John, Pete and I climbed some more lovely mountains, and there was no further talk of over-ambitious running projects. The weather had been settled so far, but a storm was forecast one afternoon, so we all got together with Mandy and Kit for a morning of bolted sport climbing on a crag a few minutes' walk from the campsite. Climbing on bolted crags is objectively the safest type of outdoor climbing you can do. No need to put in your own protection: bolts are there every couple of metres to clip the rope through to protect any possible fall, and, if you cannot complete the climb, you can always use the bolts to lower off. It was a sunny morning; we were all relaxed, no worries. We were pleased with what we had done on the holiday so far and chatted as we ambled along to the base of the crag. This was just a couple of hours' safe and pleasant sport before the rain.

Except it wasn't. By tea time, it was raining. By tea time, Martha, John, Pete, Mandy and I were at the police station in Chamonix. Kit was dead.

We had been ready to abseil down just before it started raining. The storm was coming in fast, but it was only two or three long abseils on good bolted anchors back to the bottom. The worst that could happen would be a thorough soaking. It was a routine thing, a thing that Kit, who had climbed and taught climbing for decades, had done countless times. Pete and Kit were climbing together, and Kit set up their rope through the anchor for their first abseil. Mandy and I were on the same ledge only a couple of metres away using other sound bolted anchors. I was securely tied on, and, while Mandy was sorting out our ropes, I turned around to see Kit set off to abseil down. Something was very wrong. The ropes Kit had tied came loose, and, as she began to fall, I instinctively reached out but was too far away to grab her.

My brain instantly became a jarring network of chaos, and I couldn't make sense of anything. Mandy somehow managed to keep calm, making sure Pete and I kept safe on that descent. We were shocked and could barely function. By now, it was raining and thundering, and we were a hundred metres or more up the rock face. Over and over, Mandy shouted at us what to do, constantly demanding our full attention. She kept on repeating instructions as each one of us abseiled down, so that we were forced to keep concentrating on the job of getting ourselves down safely. Mandy's insistent voice did not allow space for us to give in to the devastating emotions that were welling up. What we knew to be true at the bottom of the crag was too intolerable to accept.

The policeman who came with the helicopter was a tower of strength. Everyone looked after us and helped us. When we eventually got back to the campsite, the owner, off his own bat, had already arranged for us a room in a hotel over the road so that we could sit and chat together out of the rain. Everyone, including Kit's insurers, the British Embassy and the police, was supportive and efficient. Except the budget airline, who, when it came to rearranging flights and getting Kit's baggage home, were distressingly obstructive.

When we got home, I went back to work. We had a lot to sort out. Along with Kit's family and other friends, we organised her funeral and began to sort out her house, which was very near to ours. I would cry quite a lot in quiet moments, sometimes between seeing patients. Nine minutes for the patient and a minute for crying. My colleagues seemed clueless as to what I was going through. The love of Mandy and our friends kept me going, along with something else: running. It was obvious we would struggle to go climbing, but climbing was what we did. It was what we did to have adventures, to get exercise, to get out, to relax, to enjoy life. Climbers – that is who and what we are. How could we go climbing after what happened, but how could we not? For a while, we couldn't bring ourselves to climb, and so running became my alternative therapy.

Most mornings before work, I would go for a three-mile run along the lanes around Ennerdale. By the time I was at the footbridge which led back to our house over the fields, I usually had tears streaming down my cheeks.

One evening, I spread out a map of the Lake District on the cardboard on the living room floor and had a long hard look at the Bob Graham route. I made some notes and did more research. After setting off from Keswick, the route crosses a road four times, so it is divided into five sections, or legs. I decided to try running a leg or two. When I went out on legs one and two, it was evident that I could not cover a single section at anything like the pace required for a sub-twenty-four-hour round. Undeterred, I made a plan. I listed all the dates I could go out on recces. Recceing is not just about getting fit, but it is also about getting to know the route, intimately. Getting to know the tiny landmarks, the quickest ways, the fastest trods. Knowing where you can go wrong and how not to. Knowing each summit cairn and the bearing off. Knowing each bog and how to get around it. Billy Bland, a great believer in recceing, asserts that "There is no such thing as a short cut, just ways of making things longer". I divided up all my recceing days and decided I could do each leg at least three times. So that was my job, my purpose, for that winter as I became focused on attempting the round the following spring.

I would normally do these runs on my own, and something about the hours and hours of just being out there gave me an inner steadiness. If I needed to cry, I would cry. If I needed to be sad, I would be sad. There is such a freedom in it. Just going on a journey from A to B on my own feet. Mandy recalls that I became obsessed by route details. I would seek out people who knew the route and quiz them endlessly. What is the best way around the bog at Hare Crag? Which side of the fence down Great Calva? The best place to cross the Caldew? Better to take the ridge or the gully off Blencathra? etc, etc, etc. And that's just leg one.

In the winter, I would get up early and be out well before dawn to make the most of any daylight. Mandy would also get up at ungodly hours to drop me off in the dark at whichever bit I was doing and pick me up later in the afternoon somewhere else. Sometimes, I would find companions but mostly not.

The winter progressed, and I became engrossed in my purpose. Kit had died through making a simple mistake. Such a shocking, cruel and seemingly random event. Kit had been one of Mandy's closest friends for decades. When we moved from Yorkshire to the Lakes, Kit came too and bought a house a couple of miles from us. Life would never be the same again. Although life is never the same. Every day we live changes us, but trauma and grief require healing. When I reflect on it, I realise that I have never known anyone to recover from grief and trauma, or any other emotional hardships for that matter, without doing something about it. Psychological recovery is a practical matter; it's not really about sitting in a chair and being empathised with. Sometimes it can be helpful to talk about our feelings yet often simply talking is not enough.

I realised my grief needed space and time. Grief has its own timescale, and, although it can be needlessly prolonged, it cannot be hurried. People have measured physiological parameters such as hormone levels, blood pressure and sleep patterns in the grief-stricken, and it takes months, or sometimes up to a couple of years, to get back to normal. Our biology betrays what kind of animal we are. We are an animal that needs friends, needs love, needs to belong. We will seek those things out because we cannot function properly without them, and, when we lose them, it hurts.

I was not thinking about the accident and Kit all the time I was out on recces, although I did at times. I was absorbed in the route, concentrating on the hills and just being out and running. Trying to stretch my imagination to believe I could put all five legs together in one run lasting under twenty-four hours. This would be a big stretch, as I was coming back exhausted after running just one leg. Gradually, my times improved, and, towards the end of the winter, I ran a couple of double legs.

I can still remember certain times on those recces as if they were photographs, detailed pictures in my brain. Sunrises on Skiddaw and snowy trods over the Dodds. Ice on Grisedale Tarn and mist swirling over Bowfell. The feeling of wildness standing on Steeple like an eagle on a perch, overlooking the Ennerdale valley. Once nearly killing myself sliding down steep ice on the side of Pillar in my fell shoes and in a gale, when I should have had an ice axe and crampons. I was learning the route, the way, and the ways and moods of these fells. I had recently watched a wonderful film called *Unbranded* about four young cowboys riding wild mustang horses from Mexico to Canada. They wanted to draw attention to the plight of the horses and the terrible loss of their wild environment. One of the boys remarked: "There's not enough room out there for these horses anymore, and sometimes it feels as though there's not enough room for us." In the past, I had felt it myself, this terrible sensation of being boxed in, but at last I was now living in a place where I had plenty of room. During these beautiful wild days on the fells, I began to feel strong and fit and excited.

Climbing was a struggle. Trauma has an anatomy different from grief. Trauma often has the effect of switching on the fight-or-flight mechanism in response to a certain situation or memory and this can happen so fast that one's thinking brain does not have time to intervene. It is obvious why this response has evolved and why it is so powerful in a species like us. If we did not have a reliable biological mechanism for getting out of danger fast, we would never have survived. Dangerous situations must be instantly recognised and reacted to. Our self-preserving instinctual brain wants to hold onto memories associated with threatening events and code them as dangerous in case a similar thing happens again. That's no good, though, when you want to drive a car again after a crash, make love after having been raped or, for us, to climb again after the accident and not be disabled with terror. Some memories need recoding; otherwise, they can haunt you forever.

One of the theories about why mental-health problems are so common, and on the increase, is that our modern environment abounds in threat signals which keep us in a state of high alert. Our environment induces stress in a way we have not adapted to cope with, which is why it is easy for us to forget how to truly relax and feel safe. If the stress chemicals involved in flight-or-fight reactions are constantly running through us, we cannot rest or repair, which inevitably affects health. Responses to specific traumas are testament to how powerful our biological instincts are. No matter how much Mandy and I wanted to climb, whenever we approached a crag, we would feel sick, shaky and panicky, believing it was all out of control. The first time we abseiled off the top of a crag after the accident was in Langdale. The abseil anchor was good, everything was good. There was no logical reason why we had to check every little thing a dozen times or more and keep saying to each other, "Will it be alright?" Slowly and shakily, Mandy went down. I followed. It did not feel good, but it was a start. We developed some strategies, though, which I suppose a behavioural psychologist might describe as *graded exposure*. We climbed easy routes and stopped and belayed as often as we wanted, sometimes doing ridiculously short pitches. Not much of it was conscious; we just did what we felt we could while trying to keep each other calm and hoping it would start to feel better.

The impulse to climb won out in the end. It took a long time, but we can climb again and feel happy and relaxed being out on the crags now. That said, fear still holds us back more than necessary, and I have not climbed as well or as hard since the accident. Then again, I'm not sure if part of that isn't down to my attention being diverted towards my new love, fell running. It makes me smile to think that my instinct to climb has won out over my instinct to fear, and this is not mind over matter: it is simply learning to feel both comfortable and engaged in life. White-knuckle bravery rarely leads to either enjoyment or good performance in any sport and least of all in climbing where balance and ease of movement are essential.

I use the word instinct carefully, for, within me, the impulses to climb and run do feel instinctive. Sometimes, I get a particular feeling when running in a group of three of four people. A sort of primeval feeling. It's to do with the rhythm of running in a small pack. It feels purposeful and right, deeper than what has been learnt and akin to something innate. I am much more an innate runner than an innate climber, but there's something of both in me, which is not that surprising for a bipedal ape. In the urban world it is easy to lose touch with our status as animals. I had pretty good opportunities to play outside when I was a child, certainly much better than a lot of children do now. Evidence yielded by conventional measures of wellbeing suggests that the group presently suffering from the biggest deterioration in mental health is teenagers and young adults. It seems to me that there is some kind of connection between suffering from depression and being cut off. Cut off from the world and oneself. For me, playing at running and climbing creates connection not just with the outside world but also with my inner self. It feels as if the wiring joins up a lot better after a run. Running with friends along dark lanes on a winter's night with a head torch on, pushing the pace and pushing each other, each keeping a fast stride, aware of the collective effort and rhythm. From the depths of my ancient DNA to the outer edge of my modern human brain, I feel connected. It is my belief that such feelings of connection are what allow us to heal from the wounds which life inflicts on us.

There are more modern ways to deal with emotional trauma than the do-it-yourself graded exposure approach that Mandy and I took. These include *eye movement desensitisation* (EMD) and the *rewind technique* practised by Human Givens psychologists. Any method which can keep the traumatised person calm while playing the memory through conscious awareness can turn the trauma from a timeless threat to an unpleasant past memory.

Psychology as a science is growing up, and there is now much more recognition of the role of trauma in causing human suffering, long after the traumatic event has passed. Psychological methods based on so-called analytic (Freudian) traditions have sometimes caused damage, as they can relive the trauma without the necessary techniques to process it. This can risk strengthening the fear rather than disempowering it. We, like other animals, are susceptible to being psychologically traumatised because we have evolved the emotion of fear. Fear is a really nasty emotion; although we need it to protect us from danger, fear is like a teenage party: it can so easily get out of hand. For me, stopping fear from running amok is still a work in progress, but an important one because, as I so often see in people who come to me for help, fear can stop you from living.

Our lives did move on as we gradually emerged from the winter after Kit's death then on the 7th April 2006, Mandy and I drank a lot of champagne and laughed a lot with a big bunch of friends. After the registry office and a lunch at home we went on a walk from Ennerdale up Crag Fell in a dramatic thunderstorm, followed by a beautiful and delicious dinner in the Quince and Medlar restaurant in Cockermouth. It was a perfect day: the day Mandy and I had our civil-partnership ceremony. Two days later, Mandy dropped me off in Keswick at 4 a.m., and I set off, alone but happy, into the darkness for my last big recce for the Bob Graham Round. Underneath Skiddaw summit, icicles like wicked witches' fingers, eerily misshapen, had been sculptured by the wind along the wire fence. It was bitingly cold as I ran leg one and still dark all the way over Great Calva. The river Caldew can be anything from ankle to waist-deep. That morning, it was over my knees, and braving the icy flow was painful and breathtaking before I went on and up into the pale dawn light on Blencathra. I took in the winter-wonderland vista over the central fells before picking my way awkwardly down the rocky and exposed Halls Fell ridge, eventually ending up on the road at Threlkeld. The sun was well up and people were skiing over the rounded summits of the Dodds as I carried onto leg two. Roped and ice-axed climbers appeared over the cornice as I ran along the Helvellyn summit ridge. Plodding up the last big climb of the leg to the top of Fairfield, I was looking forward to getting down to the road at Dunmail Raise, where Sam and Geoff Ayers were waiting. Geoff had brought hot tea, china cups, milk, sugar and cake. What a lovely reward! It was shortly after midday and I had already done one of the longest runs of my life. But I wasn't yet done for the day and Sam and I left the warmth of the car and struck out up the steep side of Steel Fell at the start of leg three. Leaving the comfort of the car and a potentially swift journey to a hot bath required a little fortitude, but, as we know by now, surrender does not bring satisfaction. After all, if this was the edge of my comfort zone, then beyond it life must surely begin.

There is something about the light on the fells in April, when the grass has greened up a bit but there's still snow on the tops. Everything is vivid, sharp and shining. In my mind's eye, I can still see the picture of the golden shafts of spring sunlight streaming over Langdale that afternoon, every detail of the crags and the unlikely ribbons of drystone walls standing out and the valley reflecting back the sun and glowing. On Bowfell, Sam made me take a break and do some stretching to ease the pain in my back. We got over Scafell Pike (England's highest summit) and down to the col of Mickledore. The last summit on leg three is Scafell, but to get up there from Mickledore involves a short rock climb up what is known as Broad Stand. Broad Stand is an accident black spot, with mountain rescue call-outs to fallen walkers every year and the sustained injuries are usually fatal. Since we had no intention of tackling the iced-up rock unroped and in fell shoes, we made a quick descent to Wasdale, where Mandy was waiting. The café with the talking parrot in Gosforth was still open, and more tea and cake were keenly devoured. It had been a long, albeit lovely, day, and I was very satisfied. On the back seat of our car on the way home, I did wonder just how hard it would be to get out and crawl upstairs into the bath. Would I actually make it? There was one thing, though, which I did not wonder about. Could I do the Bob Graham Round?

Three

Doing the Bob

The next day, 10th April, was my forty-second birthday. I cannot remember it at all and suspect it was an ordinary day at work. What I do remember is that, for a few weeks after that birthday, the very first conscious thought that came to me on waking up every single morning was about the Bob Graham. A flutter of excitement and anticipation would well up inside of me, and I would get out of bed feeling energised and happy. I was focused, healthy and fit. I had a purpose. A strange kind of purpose, really. I was not going to make the world a better place or save anyone's life by running the Bob Graham Round. But, perhaps, I was saving my own.

Why should such a peculiar and seemingly pointless thing have captured my imagination? *Because it's there* does not really cover it. Because it's big was one attraction. Something which demands effort has to be worthy of that effort. While it would not be a meaningful enterprise to undertake an endeavour which was well within my grasp, to do the Bob Graham I would need to extend myself considerably. I was wondering what Pete would make of it if he knew about my lonely apprenticeship throughout the winter. Perhaps I was being cheeky to think that

I could follow the revered tradition of doing the round. When out on recces on the fells, I had occasionally run into other Bob Graham Round aspirants and compared notes, as when I came across Dale and Denise on the top of Hindscarth, the penultimate summit on the round. Complete strangers exchanging summit smiles on a sunny spring morning, trotting over Robinson and accepting the invitation to run together down the Newlands Valley into Keswick. After an hour's chat, we were comrades in our quest, and they felt like friends. There is no competition between people wanting to complete the Bob Graham Round, there is no race, and you can do it on any day of the year, setting off at a time of your own choosing. It's like a big family, and everyone wants everyone else to be successful on their rounds. All our successes are different and personal, even though we have achieved the same outcome. Every two years, there is a Bob Graham Club Dinner, where those who have managed the sub-twenty-four-hour target are given their certificates. It is a great celebration of the spirit of the round, something which inspires through its stature, tradition and camaraderie. It was a quest which, for me, created new connections, new friendships and a new intimacy with the fells. There was also an element of pilgrimage. A journey which demanded commitment and which, by virtue of being undertaken, would change me for the better regardless of the outcome. It was as much about becoming something as about doing something.

All these elements came together to motivate me, but there was also another big motivator, curiosity. I mean, how is it really possible to do something that big in one go, what would it feel like? Not to mention a mischievous desire to confound what had been said on the Argentière glacier. It had seemed a silly idea, slightly ridiculous even, and this appealed to my sense of humour. Wouldn't it be funny if I could actually do it?

A lot has been written about the role of motivation in sport. Athletes are encouraged to examine their motives in order to set goals which are congruent with their own values, their true selves. After all, as in any walk of life, it is unlikely a person will do their best at something which they are not signed up to heart and soul. It is said that the people who get most out of sport are the ones who have a mixture of extrinsic and intrinsic motives. Extrinsic motives might include thoughts about how nice it would be to be a member of the Bob Graham Club and how impressed Pete Crosby might be. Intrinsic motives are about pure enjoyment, just loving what you do with no need for any other reward or validation. Those who are most likely to continue a sport into their later years are those with most intrinsic motivation. External rewards are like carrots on sticks and chasing them can feel like hard work. With intrinsic motivation it's just carrots all the way, the reward is in every moment. It must be hard to continue training for a sport unless there is a deep personal pleasure in it. I have no delusions of grandeur about my running and am mostly motivated by the love of just doing it, which is great because, succeed or fail, win or lose, I will still love it. There is some extrinsic motivation in me as well, though. I cannot pretend I have not been happy to come home with a prize or two. But that would come later.

There are no prizes on the Bob Graham Round: it's a personal challenge. A few runners manage the whole thing unsupported, but most mortals, including me, choose to ask friends to run different sections alongside them. This helps to keep you going in body and spirit as they ply you with food, drink and encouragement. At that time, I had Fridays off work so, taking no heed of superstition, set Friday, May 13th, aside for resting. I had settled on 2.30 a.m. the following day as my start time in order to try to get past the awkward rocky descent of Great Gable, which is mid-way through leg four, before dark that evening. It is hard to rest when you are so excited. Like a naughty child, I was ordered back to bed several times during the evening as Mandy studied her schedule and detailed instructions of where, and at what time, she and her friend Sally needed to be throughout the following day. Which support runners needed picking up and dropping off and what kit they needed. What food to have ready and which spare clothes. As a joke, I had inserted an instruction to visit the plant sale that was taking place in Cockermouth. Pat and Eileen, my second car-based support crew, are great gardeners, and I knew they would find a plant sale in the schedule amusing.

Porridge at midnight is not everyone's idea of how to start a great weekend. After an unceremonious breakfast, we were off –

this was it. Soft drizzle dappled the windscreen as Mandy and I made the forty-minute journey to Keswick. I was quiet, slightly disbelieving. This was really *the* day – it had arrived. It felt more exciting than any childhood Christmas. The runners who came to support me on leg one were two aspirants, whose favour I would return by supporting them on their attempts a few weeks later. Our small party assembled quietly in the deserted Main Street in Keswick and waited for our countdown in front of the Moot Hall steps. Time to go, but not too fast, through the park and up the trail past Latrigg. Up on the Skiddaw path, the light of our head-torches bounced back off the fog, making it hard to see anything. We tried running in the dark without the torches on. Neither option worked very well, but being slowed down a bit at this stage might not have been a bad thing. However, wasting energy on worrying definitely was a bad thing, so it didn't help that I knew that, in this thick mist, getting the quickest lines would be really hard. My anxiety levels, already way too high, were cranked up further by the fact that we did go the wrong way down the back of Skiddaw. After Great Calva, however, we were back on track, and it was light, albeit still very misty, over Blencathra. Our arrival at the first road crossing at Threlkeld was bang on time at 6.30 a.m., but my nerves were frayed and my energy was very depleted. Leg one had been fraught and hard work, and, surely, it would only get harder. I sat down on a folding chair, and Mandy gave me a sandwich and a cup of tea. Suddenly, there was a tap on my shoulder and an invitation from an unfamiliar voice:

"Come with me."

I had never met Barry Johnson before and did not have a clue who he was. In fact, he had just come along for a run out with his friend David Clarkson, who, along with Angela Brand-Barker, was my leg two support team. It was as if Barry had taken one look at me and seen right through me, read me like a book. He knew exactly how to deal with my anxiety and tense response to the situation. I found out later that Barry is not only a legend in fell running but also a high-level professional sports coach. I had intended to sit down eat and then start running, but Barry just made me walk down the road, sandwich in hand. I dutifully complied, chomping away while listening to his wisdom. Ten minutes later, we were making good progress up the first fell on leg two, Clough Head. A weight had lifted from my shoulders, I was using less energy, and my whole mood was completely changed. Barry had done one essential thing which must happen in order to succeed at something which demands a sustained and measured effort. He had calmed me down. It wasn't just what he said which calmed me, telling me how well I was doing and encouraging me to take it easy and eat. Barry also had a manner which exuded an unfussy confidence and he was able to transmit it, just by his presence. Then, when I was calm, he convinced me that all I had to do was keep going at this pace. Just keep eating, keep drinking and keep going at a comfortably steady pace. Nothing else. Don't even think about anything else. That was it. Simple. After Clough Head, there is pleasant, relatively easy, running across the grassy tops of the Dodds, and I started to just enjoy being out with Barry, David and Angela. There was something that felt funny about it until it dawned on me that this was the first time that I had run this bit without a covering of snow. Instead of crisp whiteness, there was green grass pearled by the almost drizzling wet mist. David kept an eye on the pace and noted the times at each summit. At that time, I hardly knew him; he was a local doctor and good fell runner, and I had cheekily asked him if he would help. He too was chirpy, efficient and calm. Angela kept feeding me, and, knowing her international orienteering pedigree, I was not worried about the route choice, even though we were in thick mist and light rain all the way. At Seat Sandal, the last summit on leg two, my new friends Dale and Denise popped up. They had come out just to cheer me on. I had mentioned the date I was planning for the run, and they had guessed about what time I would be getting to that spot. I was so touched that they had come up a fell to encourage me before their own planned run with their friends later in the day. It's a steep and thigh-sapping rough run down from Seat Sandal to the Dunmail Raise road crossing, but I was relaxed and happy. Loads of people were at Dunmail having cups of tea on the roadside at Pat and Eileen's mobile café, and my dear friend and climbing buddy Jenny Power had come from Northumberland with special flapjacks.

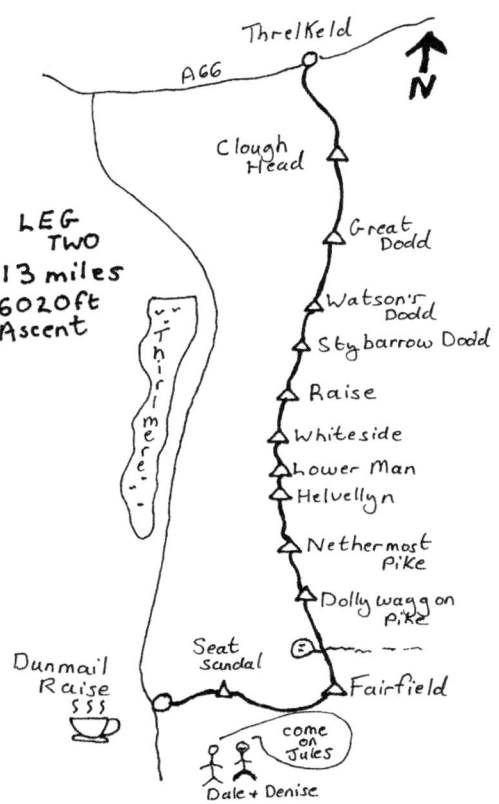

Even though her leg was over, Angela was not resting on her laurels. Being supported by seasoned athletes was quite an education for me. As soon as I sat down on a camping chair, she had my shoes off and was rifling through the spare-sock bag.

"Where's the Vaseline?"

"Vaseline? Nobody told us we needed Vaseline!"

Horrified and giving Mandy scathing looks, Angela disdainfully picked out the least bad pair of socks. Although it was me who was responsible for the ropey state of my socks Mandy meekly took the blame. Angela then lent me her waterproof top to continue with on leg three, as it was lighter than mine. My leg two crew were the bee's knees and did everything they possibly could to help me. Although it had been gently raining ever since I had set off over eight hours previously, the weather did not feel that bad. I was soon off up steep Steel Fell on leg three with Sam Ayers and her friend Dave, another dream team. I marvelled at my fortune to have people like this along with me.

I remembered my recce on that snowy day a few weeks previously, when Sam had joined me for leg three. It had not been that long since I had got to know Sam, whom we now fondly and deservedly refer to as *The Gazelle*. It was at one of my very early races on Blake Fell, when Sam was Race Organiser, that we first met. At this point, I still behaved like an old-fashioned climber, and there was a long way to go in my transformation to being an athlete. It used to be traditional for climbers to drink a lot of alcohol, and the previous evening I had been led astray with a bottle of whisky by some visiting friends. Blake was our local fell in Ennerdale, and the Blake's Heaven Fell Race is a tough little test in the bite of February. I did it with a raging hangover and threw up not long after the start. Being sick made me feel a bit better, and I managed to nurse myself round to the finish, vowing to take race preparation more seriously in future. Sam was trying to concentrate on getting the results table organised but had an unwelcome distraction in Mandy, who was enthusiastically quizzing her about fell racing. Mandy knew I wanted to meet some runners, and it was her way of trying to make friends. Meanwhile, our naughty foxhound, Holly, was running amok in the tea-and-cakes tent. I cannot imagine what Sam, an experienced coach, a proper athlete, a thoroughly organised and methodical person, must have thought of us. It is perhaps testament to Sam's sense of humour that our friendship blossomed. She is also fond of a challenge, and, in the years that we have been friends, I have often met that brief. My disorganised approach and as Sam described it, "bloody-minded and pig-headed" belief that simply putting in more effort is the answer to all of life's challenges has understandably exasperated her at times. Although some of her wisdom has slowly got through to me, I think she still regards me as *untrainable*. (A bit like a naughty foxhound, in fact.)

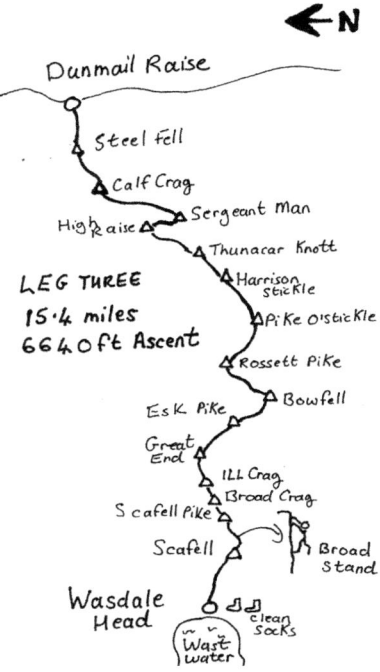

On the Bob Graham it was around Bowfell that I remember confessing to Sam that I was starting to feel tired, which, to me, was a little worrying. I had been out twelve hours or more, but there was an awfully long way, nearly half, to go. Sam decided to distract me by chatting about what to do after the Bob Graham. This was a novel idea. I had been so wrapped up in this project for months that I had not considered an after. Sam was a good fell runner and a very good road runner. She soon convinced me that we should attempt to qualify for the elite start of the London Marathon. This required us to run a marathon in under three hours fifteen minutes. At that time, I had not run a road race for over twenty years, but what of it. The mist was down, but our spirits were up. Crossing Broad Crag and Scafell Pike is a boulder-strewn and slippery affair, with plenty of leg-break potential on a wet day – particularly when you are tired. Sam's enthusiasm carried me on, and we were met at Broad Stand by Pete Pozman. Pete is one of life's originals. A poet and a musician. Twenty-one years earlier, he had taken me and my buddy John Byrne on our first rock climb. In true *Pozman* style, it was a very obscure and vegetated gully done in torrential rain. Not only that, but we walked the length of Ennerdale from Black Sail Youth Hostel to Angler's Crag, some seven miles each way, to squirm up fifty feet of green slime entitled *Dan's Mine*. Despite this unpromising start, Pete was a great teacher and one whose enthusiasm cannot be dampened by any amount of rain and slippery moss. Under his wing over the coming months, John and I were transformed into proper climbers.

Pete tied me onto a rope at the bottom of Broad Stand and as soon as I set foot on the greasy, wet rock, I slipped. My back hit the rock hard as I jolted onto the rope, safe and sound but a little shaken. I composed myself and tried again to make the long step left, but my legs seized up in an agonising cramp. Then I realised that normal climbing tactics must be abandoned and just took ginger little steps, trusting in Pete's rope. As Dave, Sam and I were leaving the top of Broad Stand to continue up Scafell, Pete looked me in the eye and proclaimed confidently:

"You will do this, Julie; I know you will."

Despite a tired, aching, hungry body, I gave him an assured smile.

"Yes, Pete; I will."

In that moment for the first time, I truly believed that I would. An observer could have described the scene, the on the rocky mountainside in the rain and mist, as miserable. Yet it felt wonderful to me because as the damp day drew on, my dream *was* coming true. My curiosity about what this would really feel like was being satisfied. It never does cease to amaze me what the body can do when you trust it.

Since leg three is quite long, there had been time for Mandy to go home and wash and dry my one good pair of socks, the ones that had been deemed serviceable by Angela. It amused me to find out later, when I saw some trees in pots on our porch the next day, that my road crew had actually been to the plant sale which I had jokingly added to their list of duties. There, Mandy acquired a nice corkscrew hazel. When we moved from Ennerdale, this tree was uprooted and replanted but is still growing strongly in our present garden. I call it my Bob Graham tree and superstitiously believe that, while it is still healthy, my running days are not finished.

At Wasdale, I was overwhelmed by a multitude of lavish luxuries: tea, rice pudding and tinned pears, a footbath, an unsweated shirt, the best clean socks back on and a new jolly band of friends who joined me for the long steep plod up Yewbarrow at the start of leg four.

My companions were all excited and chatty, but I was soon tiring and dropped off the back of the small group. Then a couple returned to Wasdale, having just come out for a short run, and my friend Fiona Garry, or Boo, as we all call her, slowed the pace and started feeding me. Boo and I knew each other in our twenties, when we were both climbing instructors. We subsequently lost touch but were surprised to meet up again at a cardiac arrest in a patient's bedroom some years later, Boo having been reincarnated as a paramedic and I as a doctor. She had promised me a secret weapon on leg four; in fact, she had two. The first was Hula Hoops. It's easy to eat a lot of sugary food, which is straightforward to digest on something like the Bob Graham, but what I really craved was savoury food, which seems a lot harder to get down. But Hula Hoops were ideal. I perked up again, and we stayed on schedule with no difficulty.

After Yewbarrow and Red Pike, there is a short rocky ridge, out and back, to Steeple. Steeple is a lovely peak; it would be wrong to call it a fell. It is a pointed rock standing proud, all on its own. As I scrambled to the top, I was awestruck and took a couple of minutes to survey the scene properly. It was the first time in the whole day that the mist had lifted enough to give us a view, but the sun was nearly down, low and smouldering in the western sky. Shafts of orange light flooded Ennerdale and reflected in the lake. In the distance down the valley, I could see our house and felt connected and homely, even though there was a long way to go before bedtime. I still wondered what would unfold in the remaining hours of the evening, but, ever since Barry's magic pep talk all those hours earlier, I had not felt worried about those "promises I had to keep and miles to go before I sleep".

Dusk gathered, and, as we came off Great Gable, head torches went on, and Boo, Peter Hemingway (another local doctor I had cheekily co-opted) and I were joined by two more long-standing climbing friends, John Byrne and Pete Wright. Boo's second secret weapon then became evident in the form of a friend on Brandreth summit with the biggest torchlight I had ever seen. The approach to Brandreth is over a flattish rock-strewn fell, and the summit can be indistinct and hard to pin down. Tonight, though, we ran confidently, directly to the beacon.

It had been a very long day, with waves of fatigue washing over me, so these unexpected boosts kept me from focusing on being tired. It was only a matter of time before this tiredness would take a real hold, and, as we ran off Brandreth, I started to hear voices singing funny tunes in my head. Then I saw strange coloured lights in the sky. Oh no, I was really losing it. I could not make sense of things. I had heard that people often start to hallucinate when in a state of extreme exhaustion, but it had never happened to me before –not even after entire weekends without sleep as a junior doctor. I squinted into the darkness, hoping that the kaleidoscope in my vision would disappear and that my senses would return to normal. Soon enough, reality dawned, and I was relieved to discover the source of these lights and noises. A great big bunch of friends were on Grey Knotts, singing songs and twirling multi-coloured light sticks in the air. My Ennerdale neighbour, Sarah Richards, had organised a jolly party to put coloured light sticks down the grassy descent to Honister, like cats' eyes at the edge of a runway. As I came in to land, they all trotted behind me to retrieve them. Then, they overtook me and arranged all the lights to spell a huge multi-coloured JULIE in the car park at the bottom.

It was Saturday night fever in Honister car park; the place was positively buzzing. Pat and Eileen's mobile café was very busy. I sat down with a cup of tea, chatting to this and that person. It was amazing. Since Threlkeld, everything had gone really well. Though tired, I felt truly happy and was relaxed enjoying the party. Luckily, Sam Ayers, who appeared again, had enough functioning white matter to sort the situation out.

"Get up. On your feet now."

Just as well: I was about to blow the whole thing by just thinking I could cruise leg five and forgetting about time.

"You've got to get on with it. Now. Come on."

I was not sure why Sam was there. Where was John? John had joined us at Great Gable for the end of leg four down to Honister and was meant to be carrying on and taking charge of navigation on leg five but had told Mandy earlier in the day that he was not well. At the time, I was unaware of any of this. In fact, John was extremely ill with a virus and should not have been out at all, but, not wanting to worry me, he had turned up at Great Gable as planned and put on a brave face, saying nothing to me about his illness and instead encouraging me on. It was not until a day or two later that I got the full tale. Having not long been home Sam was about to settle in for a relaxing evening when Mandy rang her. Aware of just how ill John was, Mandy asked Sam hopefully:

"Is there any chance you can come back for leg five?"

After several hours of running and tricky navigation earlier in the day, who could have blamed her for not wanting to get her wet fell shoes back on and come out for another ten miles in the dark? That's not Sam, though, and Mandy knew the answer even before she asked.

"What time should I be there?"

Maybe it was just the thought of another ten miles to go after being relaxed at the Honister party, or maybe it was the custard I had eaten, but, going up Dale Head, I started to vomit. And vomit and vomit. I was shown no mercy. But mercy would not have served me well at all; in fact, at that stage mercy would have been unkind. Martha, my friend from medical school, was right beside me. Martha is not a runner, but she is a person who seems able to take on any task as she oozes talent in so many spheres. She trained as a surgeon and is an artist and a very accomplished musician and talented climber. We had lent her Kit's fell shoes with full confidence that she would have no trouble with a two-hour fell run during the night despite having no previous such experience. Sam was in front and in charge as the three of us made slow progress, guided through the dark by the fence running up the fellside.

"Make her drink."

"No, I can't," I pleaded weakly.

"You will. Drink," persisted Sam.

"No, I can't."

"You will."

And so it went on, but it was obvious who would prevail. At last, after keeping some fluid in, I began to settle down. A huge yellow moon rose up into an inky, twinkling sky. Then something even more thrilling than the calming, beautiful moon appeared: the lights of Keswick just a few miles down the valley. It felt as if we were over the last three summits and down on the road in no time. A very quick change of shoes, and I really got into my stride. Now nothing seemed a problem: my body knew how to run, and I swept along at a sub-eight-minute-mile pace.

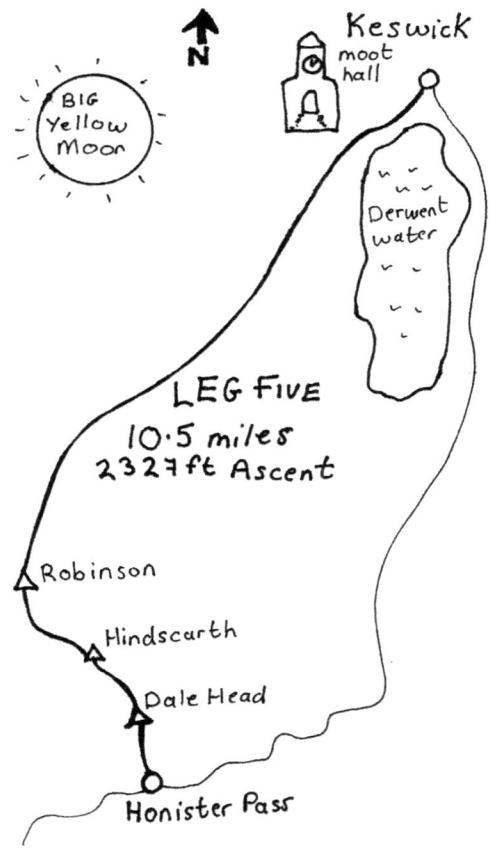

"Slow down, Jules," Sam held me back like a dog on an invisible lead. There was still scope to get this wrong if I suddenly conked out. Near Portinscale, with a mile to go, I got the nod.

"You can go now." Smiling, and without a morsel of fatigue in my body, I ran on.

Running up the Main Street to the Moot Hall in Keswick was a lovely experience. As I took my last steps, I thought about the fellow who, having done the Bob Graham, promptly turned around and ran the whole thing again in the opposite direction (a feat matched in 2016 by the inspirational Nicky Spinks). I did not feel overjoyed or overcome with emotion, but there were smiles, hugs and champagne. Inside me, there was a stronger emotion than happiness, a deep glow of true satisfaction. I had done the Bob Graham on a wet and misty day in twenty-two hours fifty minutes, with well over an hour to spare. It felt like a party, and I loved it.

The next day, we strolled along the beach at St Bees, and I failed to eat my scampi and chips in the pub, which was disappointing, but my stomach needed some rehab. When I got back to work on Monday, things were different. But perhaps not: it was not *things* that were different – it was *me*. My work situation had not been happy. I had been trying hard to fit in but was not managing it. Going along with a lot of things which did not feel right to me was stressful, but I felt too scared to sort it out. The situation was coming to a head, and, a few days after the Bob Graham, I was unable to compromise any longer and handed in my letter of resignation. The week before the run, I was easily manipulated and bullied. The week after, I was no longer a pushover.

Completing the Bob Graham had given me something special. It had given me self-belief, confidence. In a way, that might sound strange. Obviously, I had achieved things in my life. I graduated from medical school in my early thirties, having overcome some difficult hurdles, and I had become a competent and popular GP. I had climbed some long routes in the Alps and the Himalayas and had skills in various outdoor sports. None of these achievements, however, had made me feel like the Bob Graham had. Self-confidence is really something a person should acquire early on, a natural part of growing up. But like a lot of people whose growing up had gone awry, I found it easy to believe that any achievements of mine were a kind of fluke and not really a sign of any competence. When young, I would dread admitting to my mother any ambition or plans, as these would be serially dismissed as "another hare-brained scheme". When older, I suffered badly from imposter syndrome. I came to believe that my whole existence was a sort of hare-brained scheme. It was obvious that I was outwardly successful, but my inner world was one of extreme and, at times debilitating, self-doubt. I had done the Bob Graham for nobody else – just for myself. I did not have to do it to prove anything to anyone, anyone, that is, apart from me. But it was not the personal achievement that changed me – it was something much more powerful.

Finally, I acquired a bit of confidence. Not as a runner, that would take a lot longer, but as a person. We all need a sense of perspective to guard us against feelings of over-inflated self-importance. But what is not healthy is a sense of worthlessness. You do not have to be self-important to be worth something. Worthlessness is miserable, corrosive and undermining. Certainly, climbing and mountaineering had helped me to believe in myself, but, on the Bob Graham, it was all that support, all that generosity and sharing. To be at the centre of all that team effort was a truly special gift which I had not expected. It was not how I had imagined this endeavour to pan out. I had imagined that it would be about personal effort and an individual journey. In the end, it was all that I had been given that day by so many friends, old and new, that meant so much. The running, the flapjacks, the tea, the socks, the encouragement, the love. You cannot be worth something in a vacuum, and it was impossible to feel worthless now that I had seen my name in lights in Honister car park! The strength and nourishment I was given on that run feed me even now. It was not my own achievement but the gifts of others that made me feel differently. My effort was repaid a thousand-fold.

Four

Feeding the Hungry Ghosts: What Motivates Us to Run?

"We are doing drills first; then we'll start with four-hundreds. A set of ten with one-minute recoveries. Where's your watch, Jules?"

I had gone to *the track* with Sam Ayers and Angela Brand-Barker. While warming up I had a few butterflies, but at the same time I was eager to become a proper runner. It was not until after completing the Bob Graham Round that I felt myself morphing into a runner. Sam's marathon idea had begun to nag at me, and I started doing regular runs with her and her hubby, Geoff. I went with them to Cardiff to do my first half-marathon in over twenty years. Then I went with Sam to our local track, which sounds quite sophisticated and professional but, in fact, did not quite merit the lofty image conjured up by the designation of being called a track. It was a track-shaped 400 metre circuit, although I always suspected it was little short of the stated distance. There were holes, grassy patches, weeds, undulations and slippery bits at the track, and even the slightest breeze always seemed like a full-on gale there. Sam and Angela impressed upon me the importance of "the C word": consistency. I learnt about training, pacing and progression, the difference between interval pace and threshold pace and how to work on running form, speed and endurance by devising different sessions. When it came to races, it took me ages to contain my excitement and not go off with the urgency of a fire engine at a six-minute-mile pace from every start line. Despite Sam's best efforts to instil method, my so-called training was still extremely haphazard, as I would mix fell running with road running and, over short periods of time, run different kinds of races over different distances. I was like a child in a sweet shop: I wanted it all. Except, maybe, for the track sessions, where enjoyment was not the point, as it was all about the watch. Improvement would need work and track work was a job to be done regardless of how I felt. No matter how tired I was after night shifts, or worn down by the weight of other people's tragedies, if I was meeting Sam at the track the only thing that mattered was the session. It was not that Sam drove me – of course she did – but she did worse. She showed me how to drive myself, and, after a while, I would turn up on my own and run six, then eight, then ten times 800 metre repetitions with a ninety-second recovery between each one. No matter how sick or breathless I was, or how jelly-like my legs felt, the session was the session and I would complete it no matter what. It was a sort of suffering, but a useful sort. It was where I began to learn how to control my running. Maybe it was where I started to learn how to control myself. Every breath and every turn of the legs involved tiny choices. How long to breath in compared to the out breath, how many breaths per stride, the length of each stride, the exact part of the foot to land on and take off from, the position of my head and shoulders and movements of my arms. So much was within my control and I learned that the ease and speed with which I could run depended on all these tiny choices. I also realised what was true on the track was also true off the track. What can seem like chance is really a million tiny choices.

Everyone has their own reasons to become a runner, and many people do so without ever consciously examining these reasons in depth. To those on the outside, running can seem pointless, selfish and even self-destructive. Some people run to distract themselves (running away from stuff). Some people run to relieve mental and emotional stress (running to calm down). Some people run because they want to be fitter and slimmer and to avoid the modern diseases which accompany a slothful life (running for a healthier body). The last objective can sometimes lead to a misuse of running, as having been for a run can be used as an excuse to eat sugary foods and have unhealthy treats. Medical science is clear that diet trumps exercise when it comes to health, and the old adage that you cannot outrun a bad diet is based on sound information. Along with other motives behind running, there is its emotional element because it is hard work and is, therefore, seen as virtuous and character building. In an odd sort of way, it can be something to feel self-satisfied about (running to make oneself feel smug) or, put another way, running to enhance self-esteem. In other words, running engenders a sense of achievement, confidence and self-control. This is more than vanity. It is often a genuine effort to enhance one's life and to enable one to gain strength and insight, to increase one's capabilities and to improve one's health. This is why, often, the slowest runner in a race is respected by the fellow runners as much as the winner. We recognise the value of that most essential ingredient to a fulfilled life, that willingness, however fleeting, to go a step or two beyond the edge of one's comfort zone.

Racing is a particular sort of running which demands something extra in terms of motivation. I know some fast runners who actually do not enjoy racing, and I used to find that quite hard to understand because I love it. And, even within racing, there can be very different motives. I know some high-class runners who have found it impossible to continue to compete when they stopped being confident of winning. There is a lot of research which suggests that, the more an athlete is motivated by external rewards, the less likely they are to continue with a sport into, and beyond, middle age. I love racing but am aware it can entrap you in an unhelpful feeling of needing to prove yourself, and, at times, I need to remind myself that this is absolutely not what it is about. What racing does is help me to go to the edge of where I can get to on my own and to use other people to take me further. Of course, the reciprocal is also true. Competitors are wonderful people because, in demanding my best, they make me better and push me to the point where I don't hold anything back. This no-holds-barred, out-and-out willingness to give everything of oneself is not often regarded as an advisable or respectable type of behaviour in our modern culture, which seems to value a more measured and safe approach. This is perhaps even more so when it comes to middle-aged women like myself! The feeling that racing is about proving something often leads people to be scared of it in case they fail. I have often been scared myself but have always got over it and have hardly ever had a race which I have not enjoyed. After all, there is nothing to be scared of – only something to be revelled in.

Before I became a competitive runner, I had doubtless already benefited from the distracting and calming aspects of running during the months following the accident in France. I had no real need to train harder in order to improve my fitness generally, as I was already fit enough to get by without any problems on our climbing and mountaineering trips. What appealed to me most was the adventure of running competitively. The excitement of the new experience of finding out what it would be like to train consistently. I had done a few races, but what would it feel like if I did some structured training too? What would it feel like to have self-discipline? Could I manage it, and how well, and in what ways, would it change me? Sam and Geoff encouraged me, telling me that I could do well. This was a big contrast to when I started climbing, when everyone, justifiably, thought I was hopeless. Even my best friend John Byrne said I was the most ungainly person he had even seen on rock. I put this down to my back condition, which does limit my range of movement. Fortunately, John had the tact to keep that opinion to himself for a few years until I actually did get the hang of climbing. But running seemed to come naturally to me, and it was exciting to have met all these inspiring people through running, so perhaps it is not a surprise that I became sort of hooked.

Much is written about the addictive qualities of running, and I have thought about this a lot myself. At times, I have bought into the very negative and ludicrous idea that I might have an addictive personality. In common with the majority of people, I have had some destructive addictions at various times in my life. Some addictions are fuelled by the absence of a more meaningful purpose, but sometimes the dependency carries on because of a lack of confidence or knowledge how to break old habits. Recently, after swimming my first full length of front crawl, I wondered if I was going to get *addicted* to swimming, as I *couldn't wait* to go into the pool again the next day. In fact, my major addiction is tea, builder's with milk. Seriously, though, I have come to the conclusion that this framing of my love of climbing and running as addiction is ridiculous. It's definitely no less ridiculous than the observation that I am addicted to life. Addiction implies an inability to prevent oneself from giving into something harmful. Running, by contrast, has helped me to eat better, to stop overdoing the boozing and to be more aware of what harms me. It has also helped me to be calm and to have control over my choices and my emotions. For sure, I have exceeded the sensible at times, but having the occasional high aspiration and going for it, even if it takes a fair bit of recovery afterwards, is one of sport's special attractions, giving one the opportunity to physically extend one's personal limits. It is certainly possible to have too much of a good thing, and, like any other source of pleasure, running can undoubtedly become addictive. I would be dishonest if I did not admit to having pushed myself too much at times and to having found running hard to live without. But, even without it, I am undeniably hugely better off having once had it, which cannot be said for drink, drugs or a bad diet. Harmful addictions always promise a type of satisfaction they cannot, in the end, deliver, but running on fells and climbing on crags are no fool's gold: they are a real treasure.

Recently, not having been able to do much for a long time owing to the severity of my back problems, I had a sensation that life was dull and started ranting to Mandy about it. "I just cannot stand it. The idea of a mundane life." A few days later, we were out for an evening climb on the crag we see from our house every day but had never climbed on. I found myself three pitches up a route which no one had climbed for years. (White Buttress on Walla Crag – a great route!) The exposed situation required me to climb carefully and skilfully, staying in control, looking for cracks to place protection in and trying to weigh up the next series of holds and moves. With these old routes which have fallen out of popularity, you never know whether there will be loose rock, a lack of crevices to place protection in or overgrown holds or if the grade had been significantly underestimated by the pioneers! The very last sequence of moves was the hardest, and, with burning forearms, fingers struggling not to uncurl, I could not reach the final holds and my mouth went dry, as I thought I was about to fall off. Although, not far below me, I had got some decent protection in which would have stopped me from slipping after two or three metres, the prospect of a fall when I lead is never something I have learnt to view calmly. Somehow, I summoned a last ounce of energy to make a lunge and, with relief, grabbed the tree at the top. As we rigged up an abseil, I smiled looking back over the lake, which was both serene and spectacular. Looking over the water tinged red by the setting sun and reflecting the shimmering images of old friends, Cat Bells, Maiden Moor and St Herbert's Island, I tried to pick out our house on the opposite shore. Living with this kind of beauty on one's doorstep never feels mundane, and, on an evening like this, where else in the world could we want to be? Back home cooking dinner, I was feeling more reassured about life – adventure was back on the menu.

Adventure is a journey with an uncertain outcome. Even in our routine life, one day can never be the same as any day before. We can notice, feel or think something different even if we cannot do anything, or go anywhere, new. All of life's journey is an adventure, and the marathon training which I embarked on after my Bob Graham Round was certainly an adventure in itself. Training for a marathon was a new thing, a hard and difficult thing, which brought failures and successes, losses and gains. It made me undertake running sessions in a structured way as I tried to build fitness, speed, strength and endurance. This was an opportunity to spend some time in my favourite place – slightly beyond the border of my comfort zone.

For some odd reason, I think it was a matter of dates and when I had time off work, my first marathon was in Luton, a place I had never been to before and have never visited since. It was in November and the day was dry but cold and the headwind in the closing miles was horrific. It is the case with new experiences that, if expectations or goals are not fulfilled, then, sometimes, maybe something else will be gained or learnt along the way. This was how things were in Luton. I finished in just over three hours and twenty, well outside the three-hour fifteen-minute target for getting into London. But I had run with a steady effort and felt reasonably okay, so it was cause for optimism. Soon, I made a faster effort at the Lochaber marathon in Fort William, where I discovered that what people say about marathons is true, namely that they start after the twenty-mile mark. All you have to do for twenty miles is run at a predetermined pace, that is quick but not unreasonable, and to keep eating and drinking just enough, enjoy yourself if possible and try not to focus on what's coming. What is coming is, after all, something few people would look forward to. For each and every one of those last six miles, it gets harder to keep the pace, and, towards the end, it feels as if the engine is running on fumes. About a mile before the end of Lochaber, the route crosses a pedestrian bridge over a railway track. You know, the metal ones with steps. Steps! At that point, steps are enough to break you. Just after the agony of the railway bridge an enthusiastic marshal in a rain soaked high-viz coat shouted from under his hood: "Run for your life lassie!!" I dutifully complied and found the strength in my legs to put a spurt on, running to the finish over the slithery muddy Fort William shinty pitch to cross the line in a downpour. Having come third in the race in three hours ten minutes, I rang Sam. When the time came, I filled in the form for London and was accepted into the championship start for the following year.

I carried on racing on the fells and mixing in a few shorter road races. One of these was a half marathon in America while I was on holiday with Mandy. We had been in Colorado, climbing and visiting friends, who then loaned us their camper van, in which we excitedly set off for Moab, Utah. The evening before the race, Mandy and I went to eyeball the finishing stretch, as it is always a good idea to be familiar with the closing half mile. It was a little upsetting to find that the finish line was directly in front of the town morgue! My fears were further heightened when I read the pre-race instructions, which mentioned a special award for the first woman over forty. This was in honour of the unfortunate runner who, having won in that age group the previous year, then collapsed and died after crossing the line. Unfortunately, my fears did not provoke an outbreak of sound judgment and sensible behaviour. Mandy's advice about the need to drink during the race fell on deaf ears.

"Oh no, I don't ever need to drink in a half-marathon."

"But, dearest, it is at altitude and in a desert!"

Early the next morning, all the competitors were shipped off up the canyon in yellow school buses. To say I felt like a fish out of water would be to understate things. As we were all trying to keep cool in the shade at the side of the rocky canyon before lining up, some very fit looking women started chatting and, noting my CFR vest enquired in a friendly way,

"Geeee, are you from Colorado?"

"No. Cumberland Fell Runners."

A bit flummoxed, they were not sure how to reply. I found out later that one of those women, who had won in our age group, was an ex-Olympian and I vaguely regretted my lack of social skills on the start line. By mile ten, I also deeply regretted my non-drinking policy and started desperately trying to gulp from a garden hose which was there to provide a cooling spray. The winding road through the orange rocky canyon was spectacular but the dry heat and lack of oxygen were sapping to say the least. As I stumbled over the finish line, too weak to get the lid off the water bottle I had been handed, I thrust it at an unsuspecting stranger, imploring them to "get it off". I doubt if they understood my mumbled English accent, but the gesture was obvious and they quickly obliged. Mandy reassured me later that all the spectators had been earnestly urged over the PA system to make the runners drink. Despite having sprained my ankle a few days before the race and getting my tactics (what tactics?) all wrong, I did enjoy it and was pleased with how I had done. We made the most of the rest of our holiday, climbing, canoeing, mountain biking and even going wild with some off-road four-wheel driving, but that's another story.

In some ways, I do like road running because all you have to do is train and run. You don't have to worry about getting lost or finding the quickest lines, as you do on the fells. In big road races, there is a blue line marking the shortest trajectory, so no thinking is required. However difficult the weather can be on a road race, it's nothing to what you can get on the fells, where sometimes you might even need ski goggles to have a hope of seeing your own feet. On the road, it is definitely a more level playing field. On the fells, it's not easy to compare times from the same race in different years, as conditions can vary so much. But, on the road, a personal best is a personal best, and, even if somebody beats you despite the fact that you have run a fast race, it's still a good result. So, yes, in some ways the road has attractions, but there are also many downsides. Chief among these is that it simply is not the fell. It's not the tussock, the bog and the rocks. It's not wild and untamed, and it does not give you that *being out there* feeling. Road running is tame, commercialised and controlled. The fell runner Boff Whalley has written a whole book on this single point, and, although I do not share his disdain for the road runner, I get his point of view. Indeed, there is research to suggest that the health benefits of running in a natural environment, particularly among trees, are measurably better than those of running in an urban environment. One fascinating study has shown a stronger cellular immune system in countryside-based runners, and it is not clear if this is because of bad chemicals emanating from the city or good chemicals given off by the trees or is indeed an example of the health-promoting effects of calm and happy emotions.

During training for the London Marathon, I questioned my motives and felt a bit confused. Wouldn't it be nice to run under three hours? That was the obvious target and it was within my grasp. I had run an hour twenty-five for a half-marathon in Inverness a few weeks previously, and it had not felt that hard. But was this what it boiled down to: just running along a tarmac road at a metronomic pace? Sometimes in Christmas crackers, you get those games with little balls in a plastic container, and you have to roll the balls about to get them all seated in little holes at the same time. Such a pointless yet compulsive distraction: it's hard to put the stupid thing down until all the balls are in the holes. Was trying to run a marathon in under three hours the same sort of thing, a silly distraction I was compelled to get the better of? I still remain unsure if I can answer that honestly. On the whole, probably not. I loved the hard training runs and the pushing to get better, feeling the strength and endurance of my body grow from week to week. But, in the end, a little bit yes. Under or over three hours would have no more consequence than getting some balls into holes.

Recently, I joined some friends on a yoga weekend at a Buddhist monastery in Scotland. Although the weekend was meant to be non-religious, there was a question-and-answer session about Buddhism one evening. My question was about pursuing ego-driven goals as a way to self-fulfilment, and the answer was much more illuminating than I was expecting. There ensued a discussion about *feeding the hungry ghosts*, which was really a metaphor for a vain, unsatisfying attempt to feed insatiable and unpleasant emotions. It seems that the more the ghosts are fed the greedier they become, which brings us back to addiction. Why this discussion was so deeply illuminating for me was that I understood at last that running was not ghost food and that my true experience, the very essence of me, did not bear out this analogy. Addictions and feeding hungry ghosts never lead to satisfaction because there is little effort involved and only the illusion of a reward. Running, by contrast, requires proper effort and gives rewards which are real. The realisation that, in my own philosophy, goals and ambitions are simply motivators which often lead to rich experiences and are nothing to be ashamed of was a great relief. When I started racing, I at times suffered from a sort of internalised guilt about doing something competitive. After all, I do not believe that life is about winning and losing, so what is it about then, this loving to race? It's a motivator to experience. To experience running faster, trying harder. To experience what happens, and how it feels, when you are fully switched on, focused, energised. It's a motivator to do better than my best, give more than I have got and so expand my own horizons. The hungry-ghosts' conversation did the opposite to what I had expected. I expected to feel humbled and put right about my unwholesomely competitive streak. Instead, I was able to drop the guilt and, in fact, recognise the value of reaching for things outside my grasp.

When I ran in London, the championship start consisted of a dozen or two professional athletes and about a hundred and fifty good club runners with qualifying times. We had a different start time, about half an hour before everyone else. The idea is that the elite men start at the front of the main pack and catch the elite women up some place near the finish line. The start was a bit weird. We had our own field with our own portaloos with neatly arranged vases of fresh flowers next to the soap! A very butch woman, who reminded me of my old PE teacher, used a ruler to measure the writing on all our clothing, as letters above a certain size were not permitted on the clothing of championship runners unless they were logos of the official sponsors. Numerous runners emerged from the scrutinisation tent applying gaffer tape over various logos, including those on socks. I had to bear the weight of a large patch of tape over my gel pouch.

Being on the telly and all that flowers-in-the-toilet stuff was quite fun but a bit awesome. Unfortunately Sam was not there with me as I had hoped, but my nerves were settled by meeting a runner I knew from the Eden Valley Club in Cumbria, Karen Bridge. Karen's friendly instructions, "Just come and stand here next to me, Julie," calmed me down on the start line, and, thankfully, I managed to resist the temptation to run off in the lead for a moment of glory. The race went along at my planned pace until I nearly had to stop at about mile twenty-two, as the pain in my back became too nasty to handle, and I began to wonder what I was doing to myself. Miserably I tried to run on, getting a moment of shelter from the rain as the route went through a dingy underpass. Leaning over to one side seemed to ease things a little, enough to shuffle through the last miles. Cold, wet London was all shades of grey, and I felt sapped by the lifeless environment. With no other runners around me, I was in a low way until, suddenly, I was shocked back to life when the leading men overtook me. I simply could not compute their speed. Just why had a bunch of 800 metre runners just shot past? I wrestled with myself inside: should I, indeed could I, carry on? The desire for this to end as soon as possible held me up through the grinding pain, and, eventually as I approached the finishing turn into the Mall, I gave myself a pep talk out loud.

"Right now, straighten up. You don't want to be on the telly looking like a cripple."

I straightened up and ran in – only to be dragged off to the medical tent immediately. Later, I was shocked when I saw the footage of the finish, which showed that my version of straight was really so very wonky! No dignity spared, my rain-soaked vest and shorts were whipped off as I received treatment and took strong painkillers. Thankfully, one of the marshals had kindly located my kit bag, and I emerged clothed and smiling as I greeted Mandy and her family.

"Three hours four minutes, Jules, well done."

Was I pleased? Somewhat, but not hugely. Sure, I was grateful for the experience, but, at the same time, I was hungry, in pain and, deep down, very worried about my back. Would I do it again? Maybe.

Now was not the time to be making plans for the future, and we went for food and tea. I was not sure what to think overall, but I knew one thing: I wanted my back pain to improve so that I could run on the fells again.

I have not run a marathon since then. I tried the following year, and, despite running perfectly paced sub seven-minute miles, I suddenly collapsed at mile fifteen. I felt as if a London bus had run over my head and was in hospital with a viral infection for a few days. It was as if London and I never really got onto the same wavelength.

Maybe there is a hint of a lingering ghost in my relationship with marathon running, but it is only a very slight presence which does not really haunt me. The thing about road running is that it's great when you run well and do well (external motivation) and can revel in the sheer joy and simplicity of running fast and smoothly (intrinsic motivation). Training for the road involves such a lot of measuring yourself, and, sometimes, the time becomes the overwhelming purpose. Then, when the pace starts getting slower, the enterprise can seem a bit pointless. It is easy to lose interest and motivation and to tell oneself to be satisfied with past achievements, as there's no realistic chance of bettering them, even though this is missing the point, the point being the experience and not the outcome. Like a childhood dare, the goal simply acts as an encouragement, a provocation to summon up one's courage and energy and to enable one to focus and thus flow. I can honestly say that, for me, the best moments of running on the road can be as good as those on the fells. When everything is going perfectly the pure, unadulterated experience of total effort is a beautiful feeling. It's just that the other ninety-nine percent of the time, the fells have so much more to offer. I am not sure if I would enjoy a road race in which I could not run well – which indicates that, on the road, I am more spurred by extrinsic motivation. But racing on the fells feels different; it is something so special that even to come last in any fell race would be way better than being a spectator. Running on the fells is, in fact, so special that it is its own reward – and a unique experience every time you go out.

Five

The Team

It's not just the fells that draw me back to fell running, it's the runners: team-mates and competitors. There is nothing quite like the fell running community. Being a part of a team is special. I found this out not long after I had joined Keswick Athletic Club and was invited to run on the womens' team for the British Fell Relays, organised by the Fell Running Association. This annual event, widely referred to as the FRAs, takes place at the end of every season in October. The venue is different every year, but the atmosphere is always amazing. It's a huge event. Many runners are tired at the end of a long season, and some teams often have to deploy substitutes, as runners can easily get injured or ill at this time of year. But one thing is never lacking – team spirit. Everyone is desperate to do their very best for their team. Many fell running clubs have a long and distinguished history, and others are less well established but still keen to make a mark. Whatever the history or type of team you are on, if you are picked for the FRAs you will run as if you mean it and try your best. Our former captain Jo Gillyon summed it up with her motto for our team: "Run like a F***er!" (abbreviated to RLF in polite company).

This being October, the weather is often challenging, and the relays can be held in far-flung and unfamiliar places, so it is not always possible to get a look at the route beforehand. There is also what is known as *the nav leg*, where a pair of runners have no idea of their course until handed the map just beyond their start line. The other legs have pre-known checkpoints. There is *the long leg*, again run by a pair who must stay together, and two shorter solo legs, which makes a team of six in all. With hundreds of excited teams and all their supporters, it feels like a festival where everyone is on a drug free high. There is also a lot of time spent when others are running and you are either finished or waiting to start, so it's a great chance to socialise. The FRAs are an all-day affair.

My first relay for Keswick was held in Fife, north of Edinburgh. I had to be up at 4 a.m. to rendezvous with the team minibus an hour later. On the long leg, I was paired with Cat Evans, a younger, faster, more talented runner than myself, and we were off first. You have to carry some basics in a bum bag, such as hat, gloves, waterproofs and the dibber, which is a little gadget which records the time of reaching each checkpoint. Cat and I had to get into our race kit in the minibus as we pulled into the carpark, arriving only just in time for the start with no chance to warm up. Nonetheless we had a good run and at the end of our leg we were well inside the top ten teams. A friend from Perth was there to cheer us in and since I had not seen her for a while, we went off for a woodland walk and visited a café for lunch. Upon our return to the fray, we were surprised to see that there still seemed to be hours left. That day, we had Pip on the final leg for our team. A British and English Champion and an international star, Pippa Maddams is a really high-class athlete and a lovely team-mate. Even so, the overall standard of runners at the FRAs is such that our team was not expecting to get a medal. Some teams abound with stars, international runners and highly trained elites. We had Pip, and then there was the rest of us. We were there for the sheer fun of it. The story, though, is best told by the following poem, which I wrote just after the race.

Relay Replay

The bus that we all went in

was driven up by Quentin,

in the middle of the night,

by Edinburgh it was light.

But when we disembarked in Fife

bewilderment was rife,

where's the dibber, where's my hat?

How will I ever keep up with Cat?

As we charged off up the field

my body simply would not yield

to demands to run, to run, run faster,

I felt like a disaster.

But things did soon seem to improve

as we got into the groove,

trods and tussocks on and on

until our leg was safely done.

Then it was ready steady go
for our brave strong captain, Jo.
Leg two looked brutal steep and hard
but Jo's legs covered every yard,
not once but twice up to the summit,
not much descent, more like a plummet.

Excitement mounted as we knew
that teams in front of us were few
and times were close and we were strong
as Helen and Sarah were next on.
Off they went to navigate
while we drank tea and sarnies ate,
and wished and prayed they'd not be late
while other teams came in through the gate.

We willed and willed them to appear
but when they came, we were in fear.
They'd run so well and read the map
but there still was a worrying gap
between us and teams in front -
could Pippa pull a special stunt?

We know she's fast,
we know she's great
but could she run at such a rate
to put us up in the top three?

We ate more sarnies, drank more tea.

And how long now, and how long now?

And how long now, and how long now?

As time stood still and we did wait

but it's all over - it's too late!

Down to the finish came HBT,

then soon behind came Carnethy.

Our hearts fell flat as Kendal appeared,

this was just as we had feared.

Then my heart began to skip as

someone shouted "Here comes Pip!"

Down she flew the green and yellow,

we went mad but Pip was mellow.

The gap was still too big it seemed

along the lane, we yelled and screamed.

Then my jaw dropped to the ground

as in the field Pip sprinted round

and overtook and ran right in

when Jo's face turned to one big grin.

And we felt proud and we felt fine,

we got our medals and some wine

then got back in the bus we'd went in

and it was driven back by Quentin

That bronze was my first medal of any sort in a national competition. While I have won several more personal and team medals at English and British Championships since then, and even one at a World Championship race, not one of them has made me smile so much as this first medal with Keswick. The following week, be that at work or just going about everyday things, I would suddenly realise that there was this great big Cheshire-cat grin on my face. It could not be wiped off, although, in consultations, I had to make an effort to forget our triumph and focus on what I was there for. Cat also admitted later that she had been afflicted by the post-relay grin.

The other affliction after the relay was that I couldn't talk very much owing to being very hoarse. As proceedings came to a close, the whole team stood on the corner of the woods just before the finish for what seemed like an eternity. When Pip appeared, we really screamed at her. We almost demolished a dry-stone wall leaping up to see her race round the finishing field. It was only when going round the final field with a very short distance left that she overtook others, but, all the while, she absolutely knew she would overtake: she just timed it to perfection. Those were the things I could see in Pip. Calm under pressure, in charge and having a plan which she knew would work. And not just a rational type of knowing but a deep emotional confidence. I could see that proper athletes were different beasts and wondered how. How do you get to be like that?

Things have always been fun with the Keswick team. Nobody would be upset if someone had a bad run, and we are all keen to look after, and do the best by, each other. We absolutely love it when we do well, but, in many ways, we always do well because we always try to look after each other and enjoy our escapades. Yet sometimes, we do make mistakes; one mistake I genuinely regret was failing to look after someone properly, and this was exacerbated by the fact that this person is a dear friend. One autumn, I had this bright idea that we should enter a team for the High Peak Marathon. Underneath this quite upbeat-sounding title lurks a dark and sadistic form of torture. For a start, the race is forty-two miles long, so it's much longer than a marathon. It is also run during the night. Oh, and it's across the wildest and most desolate part of the Peak District at the end of February. The only consolation is that you are in a team of four, which stays together throughout.

A few weeks before the race, Sarah Bailey, Cat Evans and I went to recce the half of the route which traverses the wild and featureless moors north of Snake Pass and over Bleaklow. It was peat hags for twenty-plus miles. Our run started off in quite a civilised fashion, there even being a path to begin with, and some views with a bit of hazy sun. After a few hours, when we had run far enough to be well ensconced in the moorland wilderness, we were enveloped in thick cloud, followed by rain, hail, wind and snow. As the afternoon drew on, it became increasingly clear that the recce was turning into a survival exercise. We were not sure if we would get back before dark. The wind chill was bone numbing, and we were soaked to the skin. The navigation was desperate, and I could feel my brain freezing up just as quickly as my body. But, thanks to Cat's skilful wielding of the compass, we arrived safely on the Snake Pass road and trotted back to the car in the dusk.

Usually after a recce, there is a big post-mortem and much discussion of what was good, what was bad, which bits could be done better, etc. That evening, however, nobody said a word about the recce. We could read each other's minds without the need for talking about the experience and were all thinking: "Bloody hell, if that's merely a half of it, and in the daylight, how will we do the whole thing at night and come out alive?" To distract ourselves, we talked about other stuff and made dinner in the cottage we had rented. Our fourth team member, Jo Gillyon, rang to see how we had got on. "Say nothing", we all agreed. I think Jo was quite puzzled when all she got was reports about the efficacy of waterproof socks and the quality of our dinner menu.

The next day, Sarah and I went to have a look at another, shorter, section of the route. Sarah was suffering badly with back pain and said she was not sure if she should do the race. While I was worried about her, I was disappointed that we might have to pull out. We decided to wait in the hope she would be okay, but this was the mistake. Really, I should have known that things were too bad for her to participate in the event, and we should have knocked it on the head there and then. Why was I so selfish and unwise? Sometimes, you have to let things go and hope there will be other opportunities, but I'm not good at that. Sorry, Sarah! I have a massive problem with my own back and feel as though I walk on a tightrope with it which I'm always falling off. It's not often that I can run when my body is mechanically settled. Sometimes, it does happen and I have a good spell, but, often, a lot of kidding myself goes on. I kid myself that I am fine when I am not because I find it hard to accept that I should give something up. Learning to let go is a tough lesson, and one I still struggle with, but letting my lack of judgment about myself cloud my ability to look after a friend is a different matter altogether. And we did a very bad thing. We did the High Peak Marathon.

Realising that none of us would be able to drive after the event, and that we needed a fifth member, Mandy volunteered. On a dark wintry Friday night, she drove us to the small country town of Glossop, where we anticipated that we would get a nice meal in a quiet pub. Obviously, none of us had ever been to Glossop on a Friday night. As we walked up the main street in our running togs, we felt distinctly out of place amongst the high heels and bling. After trying all available pubs and restaurants and being turned away because they were full, or maybe they just thought we looked weird, we were beginning to despair. I don't suppose our cause was helped by Sarah wielding a large pair of scissors with which she was intending to edit her map. Finally, we found the noodle bar. The friendly staff were amazed at our plans for the evening.

"Run?"

"Yes."

"Forty-two miles?"

"Yes."

"Tonight?"

"Yes."

"Over the moors?"

"Yes."

"Tonight??"

"Yes."

The conversation went around this loop several times, but, by the time we had eaten our fill of noodles, they even wanted to sponsor us!

Edale Village Hall was the starting point for the event, and teams went off at one-minute intervals. When we got there at about 10 p.m., the place was buzzing. As I adorned my head with a hat, headtorch and spectacles, I hit a major snag. There had not been the time for a trip to the hairdresser's, and my fringe obscured everything. Not to worry: out came the big scissors again, and it was into the car park for a quick re-style from Mandy. When I finally made it to Tanya, my hairdresser, the following week, she was horrified.

We set off into the freezing winter's night, and it was a long one. While Cat and Jo were in front navigating, I was trying to keep myself going while also staying with Sarah. We were both in pain. Overall, we were lucky: it was very, very cold, and the frozen ground was a lot easier to manage than if we were sinking into the peat hags.

The High Peak Marathon is organised by Sheffield University, and there are groups of students in fancy dress at each checkpoint. At the end of the event, you get to vote on the best checkpoint. They were all good, but nothing could top the group at the place whose real name on the map is Outer Edge. No truer description has ever been conceived: it really does seem like the outer edge of the known universe, and to go beyond feels as if one would risk falling off into oblivion. We got to Outer Edge in the wee small hours. Several degrees below freezing on the edge of the universe, and there was an inflatable crocodile (properly inflated), a kangaroo (or a person in a very convincing roo suit), a wallaby, a kookaburra – was this for real? We plodded off into the night, counting every stride to pace each hundred metres, glued to our compass bearings, mile after mile. At about 3 a.m., Sarah started on a packet of Hula Hoops. I swear she was just finishing the same packet at sunrise, when we were approaching Bleaklow. In hindsight, I'm not sure the noodles were the right idea, nice though they were at the time. Any stomach rumblings notwithstanding, we were re-energised when rays of brilliant sunshine exploded over the horizon and sparkled the crisp frozen snow like a cloak of jewels spread over the moor. We trotted along smiling and, for the first time, feeling glad that we had come. This time the run down to Snake Pass under a sunny blue sky was a lot more pleasant than the recce, even though we had been going all night. Meanwhile, Mandy had been given a fright. Having slept for a while in Sarah's car, she was making herself useful sweeping up in the village hall and made a casual enquiry to the organisers about where they thought Keswick Women would be by now.

"Oh, they will be at Snake within the next few minutes; they are extremely good, you know."

Our reputation clearly preceded us but it was a little unde-served. and we actually arrived around the time we had predicted. Mandy had been there for a while, having driven at speed up the hairpin road, eager not to miss us. On this race, you have to carry all sorts of kit including a sleeping bag in case one of the team gets hypothermia. I had volunteered to take it but got sick of it and handed it to Jo, who carried it part-way through the night before giving it back to me on Bleaklow. When we got to the Snake Pass road crossing, Sarah was greatly cheered by coming across a man who offered her a mug of soup. What's more, the fetching bra-and-panty set he was modelling over the top of his waterproofs had the exact same shade of green as her jacket. It would appear that the theme at that checkpoint was lingerie (or maybe it was just sex?). By then, my own spirits were low, as the soup was tepid and the painkillers were wearing off. I began to hate my rucksack. It was not my finest moment when, in true Basil Fawlty style, I took it off, kicked it, swore at it, told the b*****d what I thought of it and then gave it another good kicking. I hope it hurt just as much as I did. It deserved every-thing it got; it had been asking for it. Mandy tried to calm me down, politely suggesting that I might be embarrassing myself, as onlookers did not know whether to turn away or intervene. When I looked up, the others had departed and seemed miles away, heading off on the path to Kinder Scout. Good God, I'd better get the bloody thing back on and catch up!

Somehow, we finished, or had it finished us? On the way home, we were crawling along in traffic for hours, and, for a while, I had to walk next to the car, as I could not sit down for the pain in my back. At the service station, spectators were bemused by our efforts at getting from the car to the loo. When I got back, I fell into my dinner at the pub, asleep. Sarah did not run again for a very long time. I felt terribly guilty that we had not heeded her sensible reservations about running with her back problem on that occasion. We were simply wrong to do it. We actually finished in respectable time, but it was not our finest hour. Thankfully, we have had better times since, and Sarah is still my friend and seems to be enjoying her running again.

There is no doubt that being in a team provides extra motivation, excitement and energy. One October morning, soon after we moved from Ennerdale into our house near Keswick, I sprang out of bed. It was not any old day – it was the day of the Ian Hodgson Relay, which is the major Lakeland Mountain Relay. Being one of the oldest clubs in the Lake District, the Keswick team always tries to put in good performances at this event. Eager to sniff the morning air, I grasped the window handle, the window flung open with gusto, but the handle came off and remained in my grip! Oh well, the windows were something we had talked about replacing at some point. When Jo picked me up, I warned her that she needed to be careful: I was powered up and there was no telling what damage I could do, so, valuing her car, she opened the door for me. There are four paired legs in this event: eight runners in a team. I was to run leg one with Holly Williamson, who is from the Lakes but who lives in Bavaria and who had made the trip for a fun weekend. We warmed up excitedly, but, before we even got to the start, disaster struck. Holly's bum bag was locked in the car, and the keys were with those who had gone up the hill to spectate. No bum bag, no kit, no run, or you get disqualified. A couple of minutes before the start, we were haring around like headless chickens until Sara Hodgson, who was competing with a different team on a later leg, lent Holly her bum bag. We sprinted to the start line, reaching it just as the gun went. And it is only thanks to Sara H that we could run at all. That's what I call being a sport.

When you think about it, it's hard enough for an individual to get everything working right in a race. To be fit but rested. To be fuelled up but not feeling sick. To go fast enough at the start but not too fast. To get the route bang on, and so on. Most important of all is to feel good, to be relaxed while retaining focus and determined without being wound up. Really, it doesn't all come together that often. To have a whole team come together in that way in one race on the same day is a rare thing. That said, sometimes it's like an infectious bug, and we can catch a dose of on-form fever from each other.

When we went to Calderdale Way Relay in Yorkshire, we were all mostly curious. None of us had ever done anything quite like this before. Except for Helen Winskill, who used to run for Dark Peak and had been in a winning Calderdale Way Relay Team with them a few years previously. In this race there are twelve in a team, six paired legs. Each pair must stay together. The Calderdale Way is a circular long-distance route of fifty-two miles. You can imagine the nightmare logistics of each pair of runners starting and finishing at a different road crossing and with the narrow, steep roads in West Yorkshire even the driving was challenging. Jenn Mattinson's partner, Carl Bell, had kindly agreed to be co-team-manager with Mandy. Carl and Mandy had to get us all on time to where we needed to start and then bring us back again from where we ended up. As there was such a big group, I had booked us a big place to stay. It was a wonderful barn with a huge fire and a great kitchen; the only trouble was the mile and a half of steep off-road driving to get up to it. Coupled with monsoon rain on the Saturday, getting all the food up there and cooking for fourteen was a feat in itself. Hilarity ensured as we went through the spreadsheet of times, places, kit, car keys, etc, and I went to bed wondering if we were heading for a fiasco.

The first runners, Jenn and Cat Spurden, were off at an ungodly hour, and they coped well with the wet conditions and handed over in good time. Holly had come over from Bavaria for another fun weekend to do leg two with Lyn Thompson. Despite Holly having a nasty fall in the slippery conditions, they too had a good run. At the very last minute, we needed a stand-in for leg three; as luck would have it, we had just recruited a new member to the club. I wondered how poor Nina Galloni would cope with all of us lot, never mind the running, but I should not have worried, as she gave Rachel Mellor a good run, and they almost broke the record for their leg. Leg four rather caught out Jo and Cat Evans, who were not quite ready for such a speedy arrival, so they started their leg taking off their warm-up kit while running. Despite this hiccup, they ran well, with leg five also being swift. I was to go last with Katy Moore, who was pretty new to Keswick; I am pleased I did not know beforehand how good Katy truly is. To prevent the race from being really late finishing, most leg-six runners end up going off in a mass start, so we had no idea of where we were positioned in the race overall. Carl tried to keep us up to date with texts, and we knew we were doing well. I ran our ten miles alongside Katy as fast as I possibly could. She encouraged me on the uphills, and we strode out together on the flats. The last descent was down a one-in-four cobbled lane in the rain. Excitement mounted, as the whole team had done fifty-odd miles with full-on effort, and there was less than a mile to go.

As I hurtled down the lane, the cobbles were like an ice rink, so I lost control and went flying. While I was airborne, time slowed down and several thoughts flashed through my mind. You cannot let this happen; you have got to get over that finish line. I told myself not to let the hurt in when I hit the ground; just get up instantly and ignore it. So that's exactly what I did. I did not feel a thing, and, when we reached the flat run along the canal at the end, the rest of the team were there screaming as usual, so everything else apart from getting over that line became irrelevant. I remember sitting on a bench outside Brighouse Rugby Club in the rain, shivering and soaked through. Not only was I wasted from the run with my legs in cramp and my back like a board, but my shoulder was killing where I had hit it in the fall, and blood was mingling with the mud around my leg, arm and head. Someone gave me a meat pie floating about in lukewarm gravy in a plastic dish, and I tried to look grateful. Was I happy? Ecstatic – especially when we realised that we had won by a country mile. Smiley days followed. Twelve women, and all of us, every single one, had run our best. We each got a ten-pound voucher and a very happy memory.

Yes, the team is special. It is hard to get everyone together and coordinated, with some runners being more reliable and dedicated than others. We all have different lives and pressures, and we are very different people. Sometimes, I have said, or done, a wrong thing to a team-mate, but it was always from the best of motives. There is no question that, when a team event goes well, this is the best sort of running I have experienced. But, when the team is not right, it's worse than coping with one's own ups and downs. We all want the best for each other, and that wish is magnified by being in a team. You only have to experience the atmosphere at the finale of an athletics meet, when the sprint relays take place. It's not unusual for even the best quality athlete to outperform themselves when they belong to a team.

There must be something in our biology that can explain this. Of course, we did not evolve as individual runners. We evolved to run to hunt, in a team, a tribe. Maybe it is this primeval impulse that can spark something deep. I have run in quite a few mountain marathons in a team of two people, but this intimate sort of team is not the same as a bigger group. While it's good in other ways, it somehow lacks the intensity of big-team relays. There is something palpably strengthening about team identity, the club, the pride in one's own group. It's more than pride: it's a type of connection, a bond. This is something innate within the human animal, but it is almost a paradox, as we seem to need these types of bonds to be truly free.

There is also another crucial group that all athletes depend on – our competitors. After all, racing certainly would not be much fun without them. Relationships with competitors are often very much more distant than those with team-mates, although the sharing of a real race is, in a strange way, a kind of intimacy. Stretton Six Summits in 2015 turned out to be a race run in a truly dramatic fashion. Shropshire sounds a bit tame in comparison with the big mountain areas of Great Britain, but it has a unique profile, one outrageously steep slope after another, and the races on the Long Mynd are always tough and memorable. None more so than this particular English Championship race. I was approaching the finish down a steep grassy field, limbs flying, lungs gasping. My legs felt like jelly on fire when, pushing hard to get across the line, I sensed I was being caught. I wondered what exactly was happening when the crowd gave a huge cheer as I fell over the line with nothing whatsoever left in my tank. I was relieved that I had held on, but only just, as the person behind fell into the back of me, and she was neck and neck with another. What seemed to have had entertained the audience the most was the colour of our vests: we were all in the yellow and green of Keswick. Until it was over, I had no idea that it was my team-mates Jenn and Jo who were about to catch me. We had been out for an hour and twenty-four minutes, and, although on paper the results had a second between us, there was nowhere near that much. We had not done it on purpose, and what none of us would have ever contemplated was to let the others off because we are friends. The greatest respect we can give to each other regardless of which vest is being worn is to race at our best. The competitive spirit is sometimes misunderstood as hostile and aggressive, but all true sports people know that it is the opposite. To compete with someone fairly and squarely is one of the biggest gifts you can give to this person because it will afford the competitor the opportunity to be something they could never otherwise be. It is a pity that, within education, we cannot be more comfortable with competition in sport, safe in the knowledge that, as the great Billie Jean King so aptly pointed out: "Not being a winner does not make you a loser."

Six

The Lakeland Classics

A major part of my coming of age as a fell runner was running in the races known as the Lakeland Classics. Traditionally, there are six Lakeland Classic races, although, as of 2017, the Three Shires Race has been replaced with the Buttermere Round. These races are special because they epitomise the spirit of the sport. They fall into two categories: *long* and *super-long* and they require stamina, self-reliance, and the ability to run while navigating over complex rough terrain. They are well established and have a fine history involving distinguished heroes of the fells, such as Jasmin Paris, Kenny Stuart and Billy Bland, who have performed superhuman feats in these races. There is one runner who embodies the spirit of the Classics above all others, and that man is Joss Naylor. I have been privileged to be shaken by the hand by Joss at different Classics prize-givings, and his congratulatory "Aye, lass, you've 'ad a good 'un today" has always been worth more than the prize he was handing over. In a sense, the races themselves are heroic entities, and, in my mind, that's what makes a Lakeland Classic. You respect it, look up to it, feel awed by it, and you feel you should try to do it justice. The first Classic in the calendar year is the Duddon. Given my description of it in chapter 1, you might be forgiven for thinking it's held in the middle of winter, but no, it's always at the start of June.

One of the things I regret is that I have not kept a diary of my races. I have never kept a diary of climbs, valuing them only for the experiences they offered rather than as achievements in their own right. I mean, you would not keep a diary of good dinners, however delicious – or would you? But, with hindsight, I do think that there would have been value in keeping a race record. Perhaps it is just that one memory runs into another and that the forgotten details may mean that lessons have to be relearnt.

After my first Duddon, I never did forget that you do need the bearings to the Three Shires Stone worked out beforehand, that you do need to know the way up and off Caw and that, despite everything your body is going through, the ascent of Little Stand is not actually endless. I have raced the Duddon four times. The first was definitely the most educational. In terms of time, the best was in 2011, although I do not remember too many details of the actual racing that day. In terms of sheer pleasure, it was certainly my 2015 Duddon which shines out. I was able to take delight in it, as, by then, I had begun to appreciate these outings properly, especially as I realised my back problems could potentially scupper my running at any point. I savoured this race, feeling relaxed and very happy to still be able to make it to the finish in under four hours.

The next Classic race in the calendar after the Duddon is Ennerdale. As it is often held on the weekend adjacent to that of the Duddon, it does not give those tired legs much time to recover. If I had to pick only one Classic to do again, it would be Ennerdale. When Mandy and I moved to Ennerdale in 2004, we had come only from West Yorkshire, a three-hour drive away. Yet, it was a different world. When we woke up in our new home for the first time, it was a warm, sunny, blue-sky day in May. The house was, as estate agents like to put it, in need of some renovation. Sensing that this would be a long-haul project, we opted for a walk, setting out across the fields towards the lake and enjoying spectacular views of Pillar, Red Pike and all the other Ennerdale fells. Wow, we live here! Our elation was not dampened by the discovery that, at various points, the paths seemed to be blocked by wired-up gates and fences. Yet, marvelling at our surroundings, we had diligently followed the rights of way as marked on the Ordnance Survey map. Until we were stopped all of a sudden.

"I'll 'ave yeh." We turned in surprise to see a red-faced local farmer in pursuit.

"Geroff my land now and get that mutt awar an all. I'll shoot the bugger and you. Eff Off."

"But this is a marked right of way; the dog's okay: she's on the lead."

"I'll shoot all a yer then."

Mandy and I exchanged a glance and immediately retreated up to the road and legged it. When we got back to the house, we were glad to see that our friend Marushka had arrived, bringing us a house-warming present, a mattock. It was clear that she had got the measure of the *renovation* task that awaited us. As for the locals, well, thank goodness they were not all like our first acquaintance. In fact, the next evening we were welcomed into our next-door neighbour's house, a couple of fields up the lane from ours, for whisky and a friendly chat.

Ennerdale is like a land that time forgot, and, over the weeks and months after arriving there, I gradually started doing more running and exploring and formed a bond with it. It began to feel like home – not the house but the fells. I have only ever completed the full Ennerdale race three times, as the fourth, in 2014, was on a shortened course because of severe weather. But it feels much more familiar than that because I have been round it many times when not racing. I remember one Sunday lunchtime during the late autumn of 2005, a few months after Kit's death. Geoff rang to see if I wanted to meet up for an afternoon run.

"Well, I would have, but I've just come in from running around the Ennerdale route."

I think he thought that he had misunderstood: "What do you mean: the race route?"

"Yes, I'm pretty tired."

"You mean the whole thing? It's only one o'clock; did you set off in the dark? How long did it take?"

"Seven hours."

In the background, Geoff started venting his incredulity to Sam: "She's been round the Ennerdale, this morning, by herself. It's not even nice out there."

"Sorry, Geoff, I think I need a bath."

That's my first ever memory of the Ennerdale route. Twenty-three miles and seven thousand five hundred feet of up and down, not on my own but with Holly, our old foxhound, in the drizzle. I needed that bath. The following year, there was only a short gap between doing the Bob Graham and running my first Ennerdale Race. It was a hot day, and I got round in five hours and forty-six minutes. Roughly the same the year after: five hours and fifty-four minutes. I loved this race – it was on home territory. I loved getting to the last summit, Crag Fell, from where it's a really short run to the finish down a nice grassy slope and through the woods. I knew every footstep, as this bit was one of my regular short runs from home. The following year, in 2008, I was not sure if I could manage the race, as I had been concentrating on road running because of doing the London Marathon. Always being the one who struggles with letting good judgement get in the way of fun, I could not resist turning up on race day, even though I was not fully recovered. Who knows, there's a lot of good grassy running during the second half of the race, and marathon training might just come in handy.

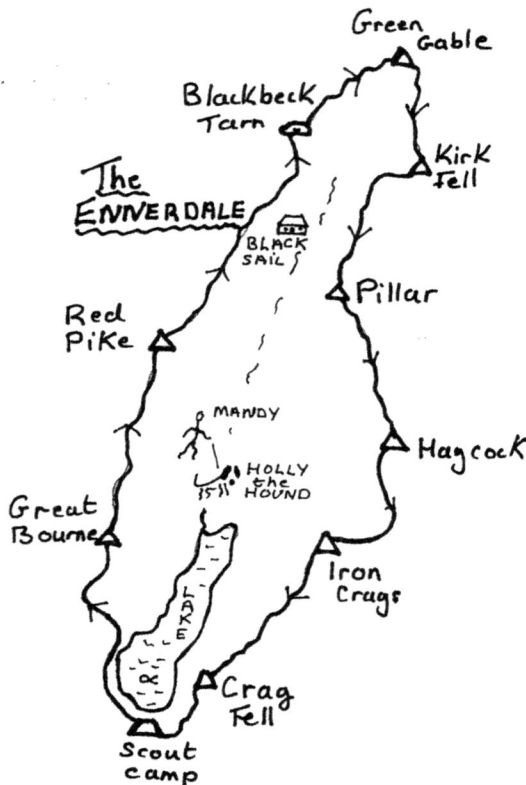

The Ennerdale starts off on a flat path along the lakeshore for a good half a mile or more before the steep climb up to Great Bourne. I set off at my normal race speed, which had become what I was by then used to on the road: a little faster than seven-minute-mile pace. I have never been good at containing my excitement at the start of races, and fast running just happened. The funny thing about this day was that it just kept on happening. I had no expectations: I was out simply to have a good time. It was warm and sunny with a light breeze – lovely weather for fell running. Relaxed and happy, I kept a good pace going up Red Pike. The ridge line to High Stile has a few shortcuts, but I knew them all well. Down to Scarth Gap, where John Byrne awaited with jelly babies, then up to Blackbeck Tarn with the reflected glory of the springtime fells mirrored in the water. And, all the while, I felt strong and ran just as I felt. Mandy was at the summit of Green Gable and topped up my drinks bottle. A bit of caution down the shambles of steep scree and on up Kirk Fell, still not tired. I could see Jane Reedy of Ambleside ahead and briefly overtook her. She's a good runner: something must be wrong here. John popped up again with more jelly babies and smiles at Black Sail Pass. On up Pillar, Scoat Fell and Haycock and then came all that easily runnable good grassy terrain. My leg cramped as I went over a stile before Iron Crag. Jane overtook me again, and I could not keep up. I had no fluids left to drink, but I eased my legs into starting up again and felt excited, as I could see the Crag Fell summit, still a long way ahead but all of it easy. On and up, and, as the marshal recorded my number at the final checkpoint, I glanced at my watch. What!? Grinning and disbelieving, I ran down through to the woods. As I sank down onto the grass past the finish line, I looked around for Mandy. After a while, I went for a leg rinse in the river, got something to eat and drink, but still no Mandy. Eventually, she appeared with a worried look to find me sunbathing.

"What's happened Jules? Where did you pull out, are you alright?"

"What do mean?"

Then it dawned on me that she was not expecting me for another hour. When she saw me, she thus assumed that I was back early because I had stopped racing and cut the route short.

"No, I'm fine. I did four hours forty-eight."

We just lay in the finish field sunbathing and grinning, completely happy. I remember that feeling of lying on the grass on that hot afternoon vividly. One of my very favourite films is about the North Face of the Eiger, which documents Eric Jones's solo ascent. At the end, there is a scene which always brings a tear to my eye, where Eric is sitting on the summit and says, "I felt totally satisfied and could not want anything more, I could not ask for anything better". That is just how I felt that afternoon: it was my Eiger moment. At prize-giving, the race organiser wondered if they had got it right and how it could be possible for me to run an hour and six minutes quicker than the previous year. I was not sure myself, except to say that road running can make you a lot faster. It remains my best ever race, and Ennerdale will always have a special place in my heart, even though we no longer live there.

In the Classics calendar, you get a break after Ennerdale until the Wasdale in July. Although Wasdale is a tiny bit shorter than Ennerdale, it has a reputation for being tougher, and most people would take a little longer over it because of more up and down, amounting to over nine thousand feet, with the ground being, on the whole, rougher. Of all the heroes, Wasdale is the greatest, the queen of fell races. It would be a foolish person who went for an audience with the Wasdale ill prepared. Even making the cut-off times at the various checkpoints can be a challenge. Race organisers must stipulate some cut-off times because, if competitors cannot make a certain pace, they are unlikely to finish the race and the marshals themselves could be put at risk. It can be a desperate thing to marshal a checkpoint on a Lakeland summit for several hours in bad weather. Personally, I was well acquainted with the rigors of the Wasdale race, having run it in 2006 and 2007 in five hours thirty-six and then five hours thirty-four. Consistent, but, by 2008, I was hoping for better. That year, the first women across the line were Jackie Lee and Janet McIvor in four hours and twelve minutes, a new women's record which still stands. Even though the invincible Jasmin Paris has won the race six times since then, she has not quite beaten that record yet. After Janet and Jackie came in, it was a long wait for the third woman home, but, eventually, they were followed in by yours truly an hour and three seconds later. I was chuffed to bits. I remember opening the small wooden gate alongside the beck running down to the National Trust car park and glancing at my watch with a hundred metres or so to go. I had run hard and was tired and glad to be seeing the end, but there's something still out there with me and the Wasdale. In that moment, a new ambition came. I could surely get under five hours on the Wasdale too?

It took me until 2013 to stand on the start line of the Wasdale again, and, even then, I knew I was not really fit, not as I had been when I had last raced it. I was mainly there for the team, since it was a championship race that year. In the British and English races, there are also team points for the fastest three women from each club, both in the open-age group and in the over-forties. Although I was not on top form and worried if my back and previously injured ankle could cope, I wanted to give it a go. My infirmities were not the only source of worry. The weather forecast was unusual for Wasdale: no wind, sunny, and well over thirty degrees Celsius! You can battle wind, rain and cold, but heat is a different challenge. In heat, you must never forget to do two things: drink and go slowly. As we drove down Wasdale, Joss Naylor and his wife were already setting up their drinks station at his farm, where the race route crosses the road. We wound down the window to chat.

"My God, Joss, it's hot. Any advice?"

"Aye, lass, dinnut burn ya feet down Whin Rigg. We've plenty a drink for ye here."

In other words, don't go out too fast and drink plenty. At the start of the Wasdale, it always feels funny because you run west away from the big mountains. It's still a big enough climb to start off with and then a nice run on grassy tops over the fells above the famous screes, which plummet straight down to the bottom of England's deepest lake. This is followed by a rocky descent and then flat running for well over a mile to Joss's. Flat running on good ground: that should be easy. It was as easy as running in a furnace, and, after a couple of hundred yards, I passed some runners I knew whom I might have expected to be well ahead, but they were walking. Another few footsteps, and good sense prevailed, or maybe it was necessity, and I too started to walk. As it turned out, a massive percentage of the competitors made it no further than the road crossing not a quarter of the way round the course. They just melted. Mandy, who was at the crossing, filled her car with overheated runners and took them back to Wasdale Head; she says she could have filled it ten times over. Although I was not finding it pleasant, I was good to carry on and plodded away up the steep rough grass on the slopes of Seatallan. A touch-and-go descent, too steep to be fully in control, then leads across a beautiful wild bit of the Lake District round the back of Scoat Fell, then up to Pillar. The skylarks were undeterred from their larking by the heat, and, although the ground was familiar, the air felt foreign. Short bursts of running on thin sheep trods were interspersed with short jogs, then walking, then a splash in any tiny puddle. Every time I saw water, which was not often, I would whip off my vest, dunk it, wring it out over my head and put it back on. Pillar was brutal. There was no breeze at all as the intense heat scorched me and the mountain. My skin was burning and my head was bursting. If only I could make it to Black Sail Pass: my friend Sarah Bailey had promised to be there. It will be alright: just get to Sarah. I could only manage jogging and walking along the nice grassy trod, where I would normally have opened up my stride with ease. I started looking: where was Sarah? I turned the bend onto the pass, but still no Sarah. I was broken. Tears welled up, and I stood there, defeated. Then she appeared on my left shoulder.

"What do you want to eat, Jules? Here, drink this. Fancy a banana?"

I felt I was crying but wasn't sure if Sarah noticed, as, being dehydrated, I might not have been capable of making actual tears.

"I can't do it. I can't go any further."

I had never not finished a fell race. In road races, I failed to finish twice, but on neither occasion was a decision involved. Once, I simply collapsed, and, the other time, I lost the ability to bend my left knee owing to a loose fragment of cartilage. Here on Black Sail Pass in the blazing heat, this was a fair defeat: I simply was not strong enough to carry on. Until Sarah looked at me, that is.

"Come on then, get going. Here's Colin the Caterpillar to take with you. It's lovely."

What the hell was she talking about? I took the large jelly snake thing she had handed me and realised it would be more effort to protest than to continue. Turning my back, I took a bite and pressed on round Kirk Fell and up Great Gable. The huge boulders on the way up Gable were strewn with runners splayed over rocks, some moaning with cramp, some just silently wilting. I tried my best to help and encourage them but had no real resources, physical or otherwise, which I could muster to come to anyone else's aid. At the summit was another team-mate and friend Jenn Mattinson, who was marshalling. And hallelujah! – by this time, a slight breeze had arrived and the air was beginning to cool off. I ran down to Sty Head and on to Sprinkling Tarn. Mandy was at the far side of the tarn, and, without a second thought, I waded in and swam over to her. Lucozade was dispensed. I was cool again and felt fine. I made a good job of the climb up Scafell Pike, stunning fellow competitors by actually running past them. Just before the summit, I bumped into another team-mate, Lyn Thompson, who was also having a good race. As I passed, we exchanged encouragements, but I knew that Lyn was great downhill and that she would be chasing my tail, so I started running, really running, across the traverse to the final plummet back to the lakeshore from the Lingmell nose, where you feel like a parachute would come in handy. Wobbly-legged, I crossed the line after five hours and fifty-four minutes. Slow, yes, really slow, but I was glad to have made it and there was no disgrace.

Mandy was staying over in Wasdale, climbing with a friend for a couple of days, so we had our camper van. The following day, I was working a long shift but could go to work directly from Wasdale in the van before coming back and staying over with them on Sunday night. Great plan. Although, as I lay awake in the van for most of the night – it was too hot to sleep, and I was too terrified to move, as it felt as if the slightest twitch would provoke excruciating leg cramps – I pondered my own sanity, or perhaps a lack of it. I got up at six a.m., did a few tentative stretches, got washed, dressed in some decent clothes and drove off for a day of tending the sick. By the time I arrived at the pub that evening, I was ready for a pint, as I had not dared to have one the previous night. After a better sleep, the following morning Mandy and her friend set off to walk up to a climb on Great Gable. I walked with them to Sty Head, and then my plan was to run down Borrowdale to Keswick with the dog. An easy run home as I had imagined it. Yet all I managed in reality was to walk down to the Seatoller bus stop. Having rummaged in my pocket, I found a couple of pound coins so did not hesitate to relax until the bus arrived. Sometimes you simply have to know when to stop.

The first weekend of August is always Borrowdale Race weekend. Since I now live in Borrowdale, it is ironic that the race is the member of the Classics family I am least attached to. I ran the Borrowdale only once, in 2007, when the route was altered to miss out Scafell Pike, as the weather was so appalling that the organisers thought that doing the full route might pose too much of a risk to competitors and marshals alike. Therefore, it could be said that I have never done a proper Borrowdale, and maybe, as I am not too attached to it emotionally, that's not so important. But it's a disappointment nevertheless (albeit a slight one), given that 2007 was the year I completed all the six Classic races in one season. And, at that time, only one woman, Wendy Dodds, had ever done all six in one year.

The Three Shires Race from Little Langdale in September provokes completely different emotions. I love this race like an old friend. The Three Shires is the sort of friend you would be pleased to see anytime and always feel happy in their company. I've run it on nice days and on nasty days, on days when I felt good and on days when I felt tired. I have only ever had one bad moment on the Three Shires, and that was down to another runner. In fell running, it is so rare for a fellow runner to do something nasty that I hesitate to relate the tale. Most fell runners are kind to each other, and, even when we don't like each other, there is mutual respect and a duty to look out for each other. On the Three Shires, there's a bit after coming off Pike O'Blisco and heading to Blea Tarn where you have to cross a stile and go down a nasty steep rocky descent to the woods. I was going over the stile when the bloke next to me came out with:

"Oh, it's you, Quasimodo."

I was stunned. I have had a fixed kyphotic thoracic spine since childhood. It's not laziness, it's the fact that my bones are the wrong shape: they grew that way. So yes, I have a curved back, which is very obvious. Maybe it does look funny to see a runner my shape, but still the wind was taken out of my sails. The hurt of this remark compounded by it being the same taunt which I had been used to as a child at school. I was downright insulted and outraged. I was also in the middle of a race, so I ignored the offence, even when he passed me down the hill with another unpleasant comment about my *hunchback*. As far as I know, I had never met this guy and did not know who he was, apart from being an idiot, that is. It gave me great pleasure to overtake him again before the end, but, after we finished, I purposefully did not want to find out who he was. I guess you get idiots in all walks, and runs, of life, and, when one makes an appearance, I generally find that the ignoring policy is a good one.

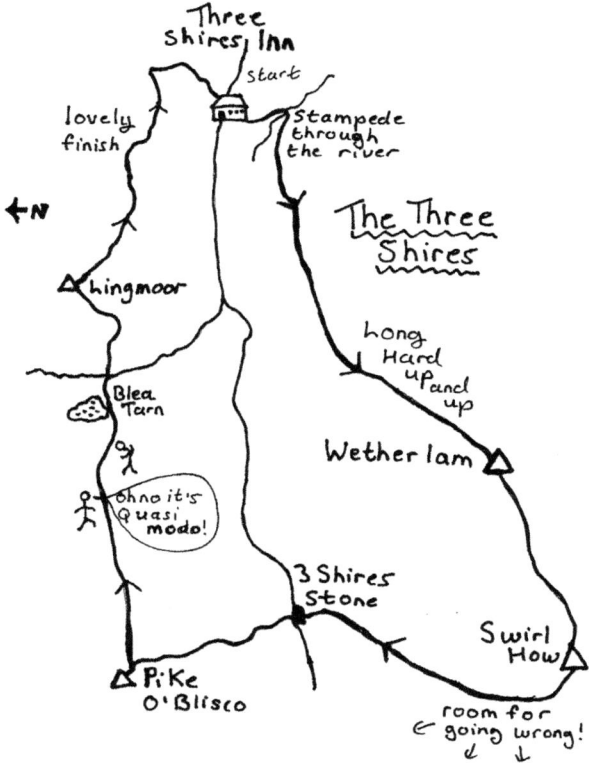

I would not let my love of this race be tainted by that unpleasant incident. Although it's the shortest Classic, it is still a hard task to run it well. Yet it's such a pleasing and beautiful route: not too long, not too short, with some much-loved Lakeland summits and some out-of-the-way bits too. Moreover, there is Selwyn, the brilliant race organiser who always makes it fun and, of course, the lovely pub at the end.

The last Classic is the Langdale. Last but definitely not least, and, with it being in October, you never quite know what you are in for. A nice warm sunny autumn day or snow, hail and blizzards. It's a funny race, the Langdale. Some people have hidden depths, and the Langdale is a bit like that. In many ways, it seems straightforward enough, but, when you actually try to get to know it, it's a different matter. There are so many sneaky bits, choices of trods and lines and scrambly sections. You can try them all on practice runs and still not be sure which the fastest or easiest is, and, even when you feel you've nailed a bit, there is still doubt if you could find that exact same way again. Well, at least that's what I think about the Langdale, but I like it nevertheless. I like it for its unpredictability and intrigue. At times, when the shortcuts I took paid off, I was very pleased, even smug. Other times, I would take what I thought were the same shortcuts, only to find the people I was with twenty minutes previously popping out of the mist well ahead; damn it! There is a slight overlap between the Langdale and Three Shires routes on Pike O'Blisco, and, right until the final run down, you can easily take the wrong line. Those last couple of miles allow good, fast running, so there's a temptation to push really hard without too much thinking and assume you are on the right route. At the end of the race, there is a road crossing just uphill of the Langdale campsite and a nice zigzag path down to the finish. It was a lovely warm day in 2007 when I came through the gate and down the zigzags, smiling to myself and relishing the satisfaction of completing all six Classic races in one year. Mandy and I often climb in Langdale, and, whenever I look across from the crags to the zigzag path, I think of that moment and smile. Old friends, these races. What is there in life to make you feel better, or give more purpose and pleasure, than trusted friends?

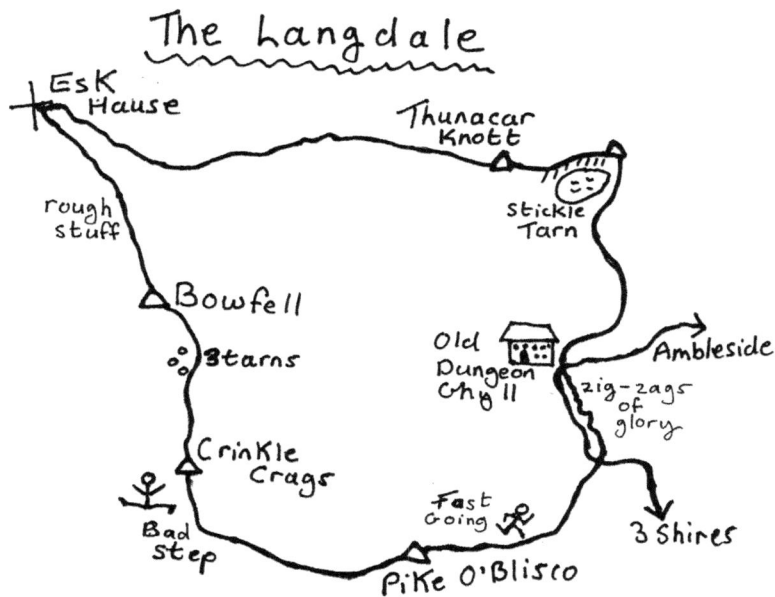

Now from my armchair, I am faced with a challenge. My physical disability has not made life easy, and, at the moment, any future running plans are a precarious prospect. But I must try everything I can to find a way of meeting up again with these friends, these races which are themselves my heroes. Maybe I will never get under five hours at Wasdale, maybe I will never get my back in a good enough condition to tolerate another Ennerdale, and maybe the Borrowdale and I will never really get to know each other. If not, it will not be for the want of trying, and something in me says maybe: maybe I will, maybe I can.

Then there is the question here about wanting to run a faster Wasdale and why time might be important. Would this goal be a narrowing of vision, a tainting of my relationship with the fells with an unwholesome vanity? My answer, of course, is "no": it would not simply be vanity to dream of getting under five hours on this, the queen of races. Time is not the point in itself, and, on a deeper level, time is indeed not what it seems and cannot be plumbed by the sound of ticking seconds. Some times of our lives pass almost unnoticed while other days, other hours or even minutes can be tenacious and linger long. There are some moments when, in the effort of full commitment, I feel like William Blake "holding eternity in the palm of my hand" or, rather, like having a sense of myself being held in the palm of eternity. Some moments feel indestructible, as if they remain present forever. A faster Wasdale would be exciting because of how it might feel, with the time goal being a mere provocation, a dare to go beyond my own limits. The fact that I can still think it and dream it gives me a shiver of excitement.

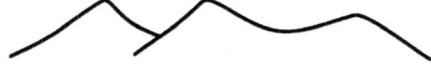

Seven

Heroes

It was summer time in the western Highlands of Scotland. Drizzle, midges and heather. These are not hills or fells: they are mountains. They have a majestic presence and an aura of mystery which stirs our souls, inviting us to explore but not giving away their secrets too easily. A few weeks earlier, I had been given a Highland-based task by my friend Ed Gamble. I first met Ed when he was a medical registrar, soon to be a consultant. I had just graduated from medical school and was assigned to Ed's team as a newbie on the wards. I had a lot to learn and Ed was a brilliant teacher. Ed is a year younger than me, but I went to medical school much later. He had already finished the brutal part of medical training, the eighty-hour-plus weeks, the endless bleeps and wondering around deserted hospital corridors at night feeling like a zombie in a horror film. Ed was already a senior doctor, and he was also a keen fell runner who would come in and tell us about the lovely times he was having and the races he had run. Meanwhile, we juniors would dream that, one day, we too would have free time when we would be able to do something more satisfying than collapse unconscious. After those days in the hospital together, Ed and I lost touch. Then a few years later at the Bob Graham Round dinner, just after I had been presented with my certificate, a very surprised Ed popped up to give me a congratulatory hug.

"My God, I did not really know you were into fell running, but well done!"

I guess all he had the time to know at work was if I could manage putting in a chest drain and whether I really knew one end of a heart monitor trace from the other.

After that meeting at the dinner, we stayed friends and saw each other at races quite a bit. Ed asked me if I could help on his Paddy Buckley Round in North Wales, which he completed convincingly in wild weather, and we did a few other runs together. Ed is faster and stronger than me, so, when he came out with the next scheme, I was both flattered and a bit intimidated.

"I am doing the Charlie, mate. I need you to help me."

He was referring to the Charlie Ramsay Round, which is to Scotland what the Paddy Buckley is to Wales but harder. Both the Paddy and the Charlie are like the Bob Graham. A set menu of summits to do in under twenty-four hours. Although the rules of the Paddy don't specify a strict time limit, most like to make the twenty-four-hour cut-off as a marker of success. Ed had done both the Bob Graham and the Paddy Buckley, so the Scottish round was next on his list. Completion of the *big three* rounds is a huge and rare accomplishment. Even though I was intimidated, I could not say no to his request for support. I just hoped I would be up to the job.

"Right-o, Ed. Which bit do you want me to do, and who else will be coming?"

"Well, just do as much as you can. No, I haven't asked anyone else; you'll do."

They never fail to surprise me, these fell running friends of mine, and maybe that's what I like about them. Realism never seems to be an acceptable reason not to adopt a plan. Most people would have at least half a dozen support runners who would meet them on the route, supply food and drink and run different sections alongside them. Well, I guess Ed is not most people. He probably asked me because he knows I am tenacious and like to see things through and also because I am easily led or, in other words, gullible.

A short time before Ed's planned Highland round, which includes twenty-four Munros (mountains over three thousand feet), I sneaked up to Scotland for a long weekend on my own to try to get to know at least some of the route. It's not such an easy task in comparison with the other rounds, which have road crossings every few hours, this making each section accessible. Once you leave Glen Nevis on the Charlie Ramsay Round, you will not encounter tarmac again until running the final few hundred metres down the same road to the finish.

Ed and I arrived in Glen Nevis early on the day before he planned to set off. He wanted to check out the descent from Aonach Beag and charged me with running a few miles up the glen to dump a load of gear at the Meanach bothy. I trudged up the lonely glen in a stiff breeze in a coat, gloves and a hat, normal garb for a Highland summer. Bits of the route were runnable, but there was a lot of sinking into peaty bog and swampy reed-matted ground. Several hours later, I arrived back at Ed's camper van, my load dispatched and safely stored. I was glad to be welcomed into the warm van for a nice cup of tea.

"How did you get on Jules?"

"Oh fine, the bothy was empty and pretty clean. No wood or coal, though."

That would not concern Ed, as he would not be stopping, but the plan was for me to get a few hours' sleep in there the following night. As I slaked my thirst with a second cup of tea I asked:

"How did you get on finding that descent from Aonach Beag?"

"Well, alright, mate, but after that cup of tea I am wondering if we should have a quick trip to Fort William A & E. I had a bit of a fall coming down."

Up came Ed's trouser leg to reveal a very large, deep cut in his shin.

In Fort William, the nice young doctor who stitched up Ed's leg remarked sympathetically as we were leaving:

"Well, you should be okay pottering round the house for the next few days, and maybe you can go to work by next week."

I sniggered in the background.

It was Thursday night, and Ed had other plans for the weekend. The fact that he now had several fresh stitches in his shin hardly seemed worth mentioning. We headed for the supermarket, and he bought me a duvet for sleeping in the van that night, as my sleeping bag was now at the bothy, and I had forgotten to bring a spare.

Other people might have been put off by the incessant rain and wild wind the next morning, but not Ed. I still have a pair of over-trousers which are more repair tape than trouser, having been literally shredded as we slithered and slipped from the summit of Ben Nevis along the Carn Mor Dearg arête. No traction on the glass-like boulders and a wind that would have you over in a single gust. About five hours in, with us being a bit down on the schedule, I took a short cut down to the bothy as planned, leaving Ed to carry on over the Grey Corries by himself. The weather improved, and he made up time without me to hold him back. At the Fersit Dam, after a few hours on his own, he met two other friends whom he had enlisted at short notice. They ran with Ed into the night, arriving at the bothy in the pitch black before 2 a.m. – only slightly behind schedule. In the bothy, I had not slept much, alone on my hard bench with the wind howling and my clothes damp; I was also worried about not being ready at the right time. I did not want to be found asleep and shirking my duties as support crew. As they piled in the door, I had the kettle boiled. Ed was hungry and spent ten minutes refuelling before he and I exited into the night. We waded off together across the bog and river to make a beeline for the next summit over sapping heathery slopes with a little respite now and again when we found a faint trod. The other two supporters were to sleep in the bothy and then run down to the train to meet us the next day in Fort William with my stove, sleeping bag and other paraphernalia, which I had left for them to use. I don't come out well in Ed's account of the next bit.

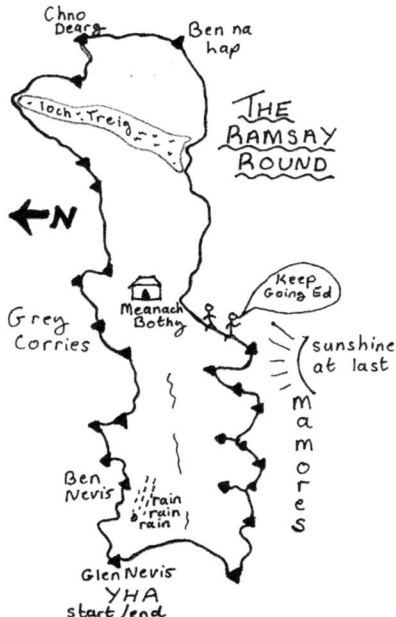

"I felt sick as a dog. Faint. Could not put one foot in front of the other. For a while, Jules tried getting me to eat some sweets and to drink and tried to persuade me to keep plodding on. But I could not carry on. My knees sank down into the heather as I threw up uncontrollably. I was done for. In the darkness, she turned around and looked at me. Then, she turned back and walked off! I staggered back to my feet and looked ahead. No choice available. I just had to follow her torch up the hill. Bloody school of hard knocks, that's where she grew up: in future, I'll know better than to expect sympathy from her."

It was not quite how I remember it, but I do remember thinking that, if I just kept pushing on, then he would have to follow. This was the Black-Sail-Pass situation in reverse, when Sarah dismissed my pleading to stop by completely ignoring it. Sometimes, your mates just have to make it harder for you to give up than to carry on. Ed's world contracted to his next heathery footstep, his mind focused on one thing only: he must follow me. People can be easily manipulated to attain goals that are not their own, especially when energy and morale are all but used up. But my tactics here were for Ed's benefit – not mine. Sometimes, as I have said elsewhere, in the world of long-distance fell running, the showing of mercy can be a very unkind act.

I do not have the words to describe how it felt as dawn came. Our bodies began to warm, and we were both moving better. As the new day unfolded, clouds were swirling, adding to the spectacle. It is no accident that those of a meditative bent relish these early morning hours, just after dawn. There is a clarity of mind matched only by the clarity of new morning sunlight. The mountains were playing with the clouds and the light, like an orchestra playing out a piece of music of heart-stopping beauty. A gold and silver swirling magic. After the arduous ascent of Sgùrr Eilde Mòr, I took a shortcut and hunkered down in a bin liner for a short rest while Ed persevered up the steep slopes of Binnein Beag. At the time, I wished I had a camera, but, to this day, I can picture it all perfectly without having to look at any photographs. The silhouette of a hero on a mountain labouring steadily upwards against the skyline. The silvery-yellow light seeping through cottony billowing clouds gave both man and mountain an aura. As I lay there snuggling down and nibbling on peanuts and raisins, I could only speculate what my friend's vision of this wonderland was, how much pain he was feeling, and how much will he was using to take the next steep step up. I won't forget it, though, that vision. And he never once complained, never talked of stopping.

It is a long way over all of the Mamores range. Nine more summits and the long and exposed scramble along the Devil's Ridge, which is an out-and-back section so it has to be done both ways. We both knew we were over an hour behind schedule but did not discuss it: what would be the point? Our point was that we were out there that day, making the absolute most of it. I was able to take a couple of shortcuts, but, for the last few summits, we stuck together. Finally, after Ed had been out for twenty-five hours and all the summits and the last long descent were done, we slid down a steep mossy bank onto the forest track which led back to the Glen Nevis road. For a second, we both lent back as our feet landed on the track, and it was like lying down in a beautiful soft bed with the near-vertical wall of moss on our backs. It would only have taken a moment of lingering, and we both would have been sound asleep on our feet. But linger we did not – not until the very end.

Finally, when back to the van, we headed to Fort William for a cup of tea and I tried to impress on Ed how well he had done.

"You are amazing, mate. I know you didn't finish under twenty-four hours, but to get around, in that weather, and with your leg."

It was the first time I thought to even ask about his leg. It was Saturday afternoon, and we were in the supermarket café. Shoppers were pushing trolleys piled high, and there were queues at the checkout.

After the tea and a cheese sandwich, we faced a weary drive down to Cumbria, where we just about crawled in our front door to be greeted by Mandy. Then baths, food and sleep. Early the following morning, I was off for another stiff-legged Sunday shift of tending the sick, leaving the hero fast asleep in the spare room. And, the following year, he went back with better weather and a bigger support crew and did the Charlie Ramsay round in twenty-one hours and fifty-seven minutes.

Some might say that the idea of having heroes is outdated, but, like a lot of things the Greeks did for us, this notion has, I think, endured because it has value. Heroes are noble and brave and have qualities we aspire to. In essence, heroes are role models. People whose lives and deeds inspire us so that our lives become richer and we achieve more than we could have done without following their example. At least I think that is the job of heroes. However, heroes don't appoint themselves, and it's not up to the hero whether or not they are looked upon in that light. Deeds done cannot be undone, and neither can their meaning in the world, regardless of intent.

One of the things that perplex politicians and health policy makers is the role of professional sport in spurring the populace into action. It is a perplexing topic because, up to now, there seems to be little evidence of a legacy effect on the health of the general population of any of the modern Olympics or other major sporting events. These events may result in more money being spent on fitness products, but, despite all this, the public gets fatter and more unfit. The major sporting achievements of heroes we see on TV and the sporting successes of our nation are not, it seems, making Joe and Josephine Bloggs any less likely to suffer from the diseases of inactivity. Must we conclude that the heroes are not doing their job? Well, maybe they are to some extent, and maybe things would be a lot worse without them in this digital age, where spontaneous, creative outdoor play is less easy than it used to be and when everything must be safe, measured and commoditised. And maybe in order to be truly influenced in our own behaviour, we need a personal connection. Perhaps the pleasure we feel in national achievements is fulfilling in us a completely different set of emotional needs, those to do with pride in our group, appealing to what some might call our tribal instincts. I sometimes wonder if spectating serves as a substitute for more personal experiences. How many football or tennis fans actually participate in those sports? I do feel that, at some point in life, everyone needs an Ed, a personal source of inspiration, such as a guide leader or scout master, a teacher or parent, a friend or club mate, who can encourage them to expand their horizons and to realise their potential. When I am needing motivation, I think of Ed and of the women on my team in Keswick. I think of the *Gazelle* Sam Ayers and of someone I see nearly every day of my life, my partner, Mandy. I only need to think about those folks for a few minutes before becoming motivated to get off my behind, stop procrastinating and get on with life. It is noteworthy that mentorship schemes where athletes can have direct contact with young people seem to have a greater effect than indirect hero-worship. Even in our digital age, we still need human contact for a relationship to be meaningful and truly influential.

The role of the truly great sports people is perhaps something different from inspiring us into action and making us all fitter. Perhaps their role is simply to make us happy. For an hour or two, to be transfixed and absorbed and to forget about the mortgage, the childminder, the awkward boss. Yes, escapism. Maybe that is the function of the greats. I did not realise that watching a great could be such a brilliant experience until I went to London 2012. Seeing Usain Bolt in action did not make me train harder or better or run faster, but it really did make me smile, and the memory of it still does.

Super Saturday. It was an evening any British sports fan will remember well. Where was I? I was at work. I was on a car shift, doing emergency home visits. Between calls, my ears were pinned to the car radio while the driver getting us to the next patient was puzzling over the sat nav. Why, oh why, was I at work? I could have at least been at home or in the pub watching the Olympic Games on TV! I do not wish to give the impression that I always go to work slightly the worse for wear from too much running. I was slightly weary, though, as the day before I had managed a long run, the first one in many months, as my back had been through a bad phase.

When we lived in Ennerdale, we had an interesting and varied set of neighbours. After the barn next to us had been converted, we were bemused to find that our new neighbour was from Colorado, an outgoing true-blue ex-special-forces American. We soon got through his rough, tough exterior, especially when we got Moss, our super-cute new hound puppy. Mike could be surprising, not least by being a lot smarter and more sensitive than my own prejudices at first allowed me to believe. He also had a naughty sense of humour. One evening, he pitched up, as he often did, in our kitchen for a beer and a chat.

"This guy I know is coming over tomorrow. He wants to know about this Bob Graham thing. Will you take him for a run?"

You might think this was an innocent request, but no. I did not find out until it was too late that the guy was an American ex-Olympian, a cross-country skier of renown. He lived in Switzerland with his Polish wife, who was a senior figure on the Polish Olympic Committee. Apparently, during the Games, he got fed up with London life and came up to see his old buddy and have a break from the action. When I agreed to it, all I knew was that he was interested in learning about fell running. I had no idea of the kind of individual he was until, in the back of Mike's car on the way to Dunmail Raise, we started to chat. He did want to know about "this Bob Graham thing" and had even bought a map. It began to dawn on me that I had been set up; Mike was amusing himself by speculating about which one of us would come undone. Would the gentle American Geoff have me in tatters after the first hill, or would he not cope, never having run on anything but a road or manicured trail in his life. Mike met us at the pub in Threlkeld, and I think he was almost disappointed when it turned out we had had a lovely run together. Geoff was super-fit and jogged up the hills without breaking sweat, but he needed some guidance on how to get down. We chatted a lot about the history of the Bob Graham and the way people go about it, and I taught him a bit about navigation. It was something outside of his experience, and he was grateful for this quirky insight into a different sport. We enjoyed our lunch, and I bade my goodbyes to Geoff and Mike, who were both off to London straight from the pub. The next day, I got a phone call.

"We can get you tickets for Tuesday. You'll have to pay, and we need to know now."

"What's on Tuesday?"

"Men's 800 metre finals. Oh, and the 200 metre final as well."

Train tickets and arrangements for sleeping at Mandy's niece's in London were hastily sorted out. When we got to the stadium we were astonished to find the seats Geoff had got for us were two rows back from the start of the 200 metre start line. The atmosphere was buzzing with energy, especially when the 800 metre final yielded a new world record. Earlier in the day, we had enjoyed looking round the Olympic Park, picnicking on the beautiful meadows and watching the big screen in amazement at horses dancing in the dressage event. But now, inside the stadium, it was time for the Master, and, because we were just a few metres away as Usain Bolt warmed up, the noise was immense. Until the moment when, as he settled into the blocks, Usain momentarily stood up and raised one finger to his lips. In that instant, several thousand people fell completely silent. It was a silence louder than any I had ever heard. In that moment, I realised that here was a man who was completely in control not only of his own emotions but also of everyone else's too. A little over nineteen and a half seconds later he became the first man ever to retain a 200 metre Olympic title. The execution was a work of fine art.

I loved the part in Usain's autobiography where, as a youngster, he had an ambition to earn enough money to buy his mother a washing machine. Here is a hero who has genuinely done his job. He has built a bridge between ordinary and extraordinary, and I have a feeling that, despite all his natural physical talent, he could not have achieved his success without that highly evolved level of emotional control.

It's comforting to know that even great performers also have to overcome setbacks, personal challenges and injuries. Even Usain is human. Another huge hero of the track is Dame Kelly Holmes who, since her teenage years, believed that she could be an Olympic champion. Her road to gold medal performances took years of dedication and holding on to that belief in the face of repeated setbacks. At the age of thirty-four she became the oldest woman to win either Olympic 800 metre or 1500 metre titles, let alone both of them. Talent without tenacity can be insufficient for success.

Of course, I cannot leave the subject of heroes here – on a track. Returning to the fells, there have been many exceptional women one can look up to and be inspired by. In the last ten years, the performances of women on the fells have sky-rocketed, while the overall male performance has not. The women at the elite end of our sport are definitely catching up with the men. I often marvel at Jasmin Paris and Victoria Wilkinson, who are so good as to be a world apart from me. And no one, except possibly herself, would be surprised that the person I would pick as my hero on the fells would be Wendy, above all others. I mean Wendy Dodds: she is famous amongst fell runners, so usually there's no need to mention her surname. There is, however, the expression *dodded*. To be *dodded* in a race is to have run your heart out and chosen every tiny, sneaky bit of route you thought might save you time only to find Wendy cruising on past, having found a better way or simply having outrun you by being more efficient on the rough terrain. Despite the fact that Wendy is not in the first flush of youth, now being well into her seventh decade on the planet, being *dodded* is still a very real danger for all concerned, men and women, elite or otherwise, in all age categories. This was demonstrated in the first British Championship race of 2014, which was in the Mountains of Mourne, Northern Ireland. The Donard Challenge is billed as a *short* fell race, which is as laughable as the *Little* in Little Stand on the Duddon Race. With its toes in the water of the Irish sea, Slieve Donard stands at around two thousand eight hundred feet and is rough, heathery and steep. Add in thick mist, strong wind and driving rain, and you have all the ingredients for what Wendy would refer to as "a proper fell race". A large proportion of people got lost on that race or were overwhelmed by the awful conditions – or indeed both – but, as the results testify, Wendy was in her element, coming home ahead of many elite runners several decades younger.

Although I was not at this race, I have heard several first-hand accounts, the storyteller usually being in a state of disbelief themselves. A week after it was the first English Championship race of the year at Pendle, and, as I was registering for this in the village hall, I overheard a conversation of a group of young men, looking like racing snakes and very earnest.

"Now lads, the thing about today is that, whatever else happens, we must not get *dodded*!"

If there was any irony in their words, it was only a merest hint.

The first time ever I won a prize in a fell race was down to Wendy. Having done fewer than a handful of races, I went with Mandy and her sister to the Lakeland Country Fair in Coniston, a traditional Cumbrian show, with ferrets, wrestling, hounds and everything. Of course, no Cumbrian show is complete without a fell race, and this one goes up Coniston Old Man. A tricky race for a rookie, but I managed to stay with Wendy all the way to the top. Then my education began: while I was looking forward to the relief of not slogging uphill and took a moment at the summit to gather myself, take in the view and spy out the start of the descent, Wendy did not hesitate for a millisecond and was gone. I did not see her again until after the finish. As I recall, I ended up coming fourth, but Wendy came over and had a chat with me. Knowing I was just starting out, she must have asked the organiser if they could not find a prize for the fourth place too. I still have my green T-shirt with a lovely embroidery of a foxhound, and I wear it fondly. After the prize-giving, Wendy had us in stitches describing the unenlightened former times, when she would be presented with endless *ladies' prizes*, such as ironing-board covers and canteens of cutlery.

Everyone has stories about Wendy, but the point is that they are always a testament to her mastery of the sport and to her wonderfully competitive spirit. I mean competitive in the true sense of competing to one's best, almost as an act of giving rather than of selfish achievement. A whole book, probably even several volumes, would be needed to document all of Wendy's achievements. Amongst them is her being the first person to complete the Paddy Buckley Round and one of only three people to finish the first two editions, 1992 and 2012, of the epic five-day Dragon's Back Race, from one end of Wales to the other. If I had done a fraction of what Wendy has managed, I would be ten times as pleased with myself. In some ways, Wendy is a tricky hero, though. She gives the impression that she is really not that accomplished and that she could be easily emulated, and, while I fall for this bait hook, line and sinker on an emotional level, my thinking brain knows that, in reality, this is not possible. That's the magic of personal heroes: while being beyond reach, they capture our imagination, and by reminding us of our fundamental in-built need to stretch ourselves they provoke us to extend our own grasp.

Eight
Homeland

The massive hulk of Skiddaw stands over Keswick like a huge breast-plated soldier, who is puffed up, strong and steadfast on a benevolent duty of guard. In the streets and lanes of the friendly town, people eat chips, do the shopping, visit the post office, attend appointments and go for cups of tea. Daily doings and comings and goings. Christmas is coming, and, as the afternoon draws on, the lights and shops begin to sparkle. I sniff the cold air, which waters my eyes, and look upwards to the fading sky, seeing and sensing my mountain guardian and feeling safe. I'm home.

Home is not something I have always known. When I was in my twenties, my mother complained that I had made a mess of her address book by having more than twenty addresses in ten years, and she was struggling to fit in my next move. Thus far, the acquisition of a home had not featured highly on my agenda, as I had spent the first seventeen years of my life trying to figure out how to escape almost everything associated with it. Neurologists assert that, every time we access a memory, we slightly change it, whether in the detail of the content or in the subtleties of the emotional associations and meanings. It is impossible to say how faithful any of our recollections are, but I do clearly remember the first time I felt the reassuring presence of the massive mountain of Skiddaw, like a sentinel above Keswick in the northern Lakeland fells. I was thirteen and standing on the pavement waiting to get on a bus that would take us on the three-hour journey back to school after our week at Derwent Hill Outdoor Centre in Portinscale. It seems to my subjective mind that I can remember every day of, and every activity we did during, that week. I remember crying with laughter as my best friend and I stood outside in the ice-cold bucketing rain trying, in vain, to get each other's wet suit off. Then we were meant to be walking to Buttermere for an overnight camp, but, when we arrived there, it was still bucketing, with a gale-force wind howling, so we could not get the tents up. Our group of a dozen girls slept like sardines on the floor of the small village hall, next to the tiny enchanting church, where one us spilt the stove fuel and almost burnt the place down. We got lost orienteering and discovered the Purple House, a well-loved landmark of the Newlands Valley which was like something from a fairy tale and which is, sadly, no more. During that action-packed week, I also discovered something indestructible and even more magical which would transform my life. Mountains. Hills and fells and adventure. After that week, my friend Tracey and I were less likely to spend time bunking off school and stealing alcohol, although we still did that sometimes. Mostly, though, we would go out on our bikes and scramble up streams and cliffs. We got Saturday jobs to save up so that we could sign up for all the follow-on courses at Derwent Hill which took us to Wales and Scotland where, for hardly any money at all, we learnt to kayak, ski and mountaineer. I literally lived for those weeks away on trips with Derwent Hill. But that was all to come. After my first week there, I just stood on the pavement looking up at Skiddaw while trying not to cry but not managing it. Seven days earlier, I had no idea this world existed, and its discovery was worse than falling in love. I looked at Skiddaw, my heart torn to shreds with the pain of leaving and knowing what I was going back to. But, as I was gazing at the mountain, its message was clear, "I am not going anywhere, Julie. I am a mountain – you are a girl. I will wait".

I went back to my teenage home in Sunderland and meanwhile Skiddaw waited. I remember that my parents would never ask where someone came from or where they lived but, instead, would enquire as to where they *belonged*. They would refer to an individual as belonging to Sunderland or Gateshead or wherever. My mother belonged to Gateshead but married a Mackem (a person from Sunderland), and, in theory, I belonged to Sunderland. In our family folklore, there is a legend of the day we all came to Borrowdale in the Lake District in Uncle Bill's car and *climbed* (my mother would use this verb with reference to a slightest hill) Castle Crag. My brothers excitedly clambered up the path while I relaxed inside our mother's womb. After eighty-seven years of life, my mother's ashes were scattered on that hill, and now she belongs here, with me. It is difficult to know what it means to be indigenous in twenty-first century England, but the language of my parents held a hint that the concept could still have meaning. My problem was that I never felt at home in the world I was born into and assumed that this meant that I would never belong anywhere in any real sense. I did not yet know that it is not the place where we are born that is important but the place we are born to take, the shoes we step into: in my case Walsh PB fell racing shoes, size seven.

The more time I spent in the hills, the more the hills became my refuge, but I was not rooted: I was fundamentally a wanderer with no real concept of my own identity in terms of any one place in the world. During my junior-doctor years, I did a spell in a small rural hospital in the Blue Mountains of Australia. Journeys of discovery are just that: you cannot possibly predict what will be found, and, on the plane to Australia, I was unsure why I was going. Australia is perhaps not the first place to attract the heart of a mountaineer. When asking myself why I had chosen Australia, perhaps I had the images of the Opera House and Bondi Beach in mind. I certainly had no idea of the power of the Australian landscape. Working as a doctor in Australia is not like the slavery of medicine in the UK. The hospital manager was very particular that all days off should be taken, and we were never allowed to work longer than scheduled. When Mandy came over for a while, this meant I could fit in a few jaunts, and, after work one day, we went down to Sydney, took a flight to Alice Springs and hired a Land Rover for a few days. The trip was a wild one: we only just survived after getting the vehicle stuck in deep sand in a desert gorge, in searing heat. One evening, we arrived at Uluru an hour before sunset. There is a walk to the top of the iconic rock, but it is a matter of debate whether it is in bad taste to go up, as the indigenous people do not like tourists using the rope handrail and wearing a groove up their rock. To these people, it is a sacred place with a deep significance, and, under-standably, they do not want it reduced to the status of a Disney-world attraction. Mandy and I stood at the bottom watching the last of the day's tourists come down. Soon, we were alone. Of course, we would not go up – would we? Until something in us could not resist any longer, both of us feeling an overpowering urge to set foot on the rock. So up we went, fast and almost stealthily, very unsure of our motives. The sky was a deep blue, the air was still hot, but the sun was sinking fast. As the top flattened out and our shadows lengthened, the inert rock suddenly turned radiant red by the low-angled rays of the sun. An all-encompassing smouldering red moved over the rock and swallowed us up. An astonishing and indescribable red, a redness which was more than a colour, temperature or vision. It was a transformation. No one else was on the rock, and it felt as if it had claimed us to itself, both ourselves and the rock having merged into one. There was no us, no rock: there was only red. And when, in near-darkness, we stepped back to earth, we felt something peculiar, as if the redness had stayed in our souls. We had been beguiled, and, as I wrote a few months afterwards, "The most imponderable part is that it is still there inside me. I might be in the supermarket, or up a cold wet Cumbrian fell, but I'm still red."

We spent the next day with a book called *To Ayers Rock and Beyond*. It was long out of print, and Mandy was lucky to discover it in a second-hand shop, as it is full of insights into the meanings of the rock's art and formations. We were transfixed, painstakingly going around the base of Uluru from dawn to dusk and learning more about the meaning of this place and about its people, some of whom we met. It was deeply obvious that the people and the land were one. We could see that to dispossess them of the land was to dispossess them of their souls. And I wondered about my own soul. What have modern people become? What had I become? I was homeless, and, for the first time, I understood what this really meant. I was filled with a terrible sense of missing something important, something I felt could never be mine. To belong somewhere.

Back at the hospital, I was not short of entertainment. One Saturday, I was in A&E when I got a call from the rehabilitation ward.

"Julie. A brown snake has triggered the automatic entrance door and is making its way up the ward. You'll have to come: you are the only doctor in the hospital."

One of the tricks of surviving as a junior doctor is to know when, and when not, to get involved.

"I don't care. I'm English. Call security and the snake catchers."
I pretended to have urgent patients to see until the deadly
intruder had been safely apprehended.

As my time in the Blue Mountains drew to a close, I wanted to
spend my last weekend climbing with my new Australian
friends. Mark was a doctor whom Mandy and I had taught to
climb so that he could go out on the crags with his new girl-
friend, Vanessa, who, apart from being a nurse, was a very good
rock climber. Mark was a very different personality from my
close friend Matthew, a gentle soul whom I had met climbing
and who had introduced me to the wonders of *the bush*. The
three of us enjoyed a great day climbing on a Blue Mountains
crag called Cosmic County, a short drive away, which was
followed by a half-hour walk-in. In Australia, it gets dark quickly,
so we packed up at sunset, around 6 p.m., and headed back. The
previous weekend, I was admiring a neat head-torch Matthew
had just acquired and I asked him to get me one like it. We would
not be needing torches today but Matthew handed over my new
acquisition in its packaging as we hurriedly bundled our
climbing stuff into the rucksacks. That evening we would have to
say our goodbyes, as my flight was two days later. Because our
approach to the crag along its bottom had been a bit of a bush-
bash we opted to go up a gulley and walk out from the top where
there was a path. At first, the fact that the good path never
materialised did not bother us too much, as Matthew was a good
navigator and Mark a champion orienteer, so there was no
chance of getting lost. After a couple of hours on this thirty-
minute walk, though, our confidence diminished as we struggled through thicker and thicker bush and it became plain, we
did not have a clue where we were. Having been scraped and
lacerated we did not seem to be making any progress at all, and
it was getting cold. We stopped to put on all our clothes and eat
some chocolate. Mark phoned Vanessa, who was still at work,

and broke it to her gently that we were not in the pub but in the bush!

Although we wondered if we would be out for the night, there was plenty of cheer left in us, and we took turns going first, doing battle with the vicious dense vegetation with the new torch, the only one we had. Those behind went mainly on feel. At last, hope came as we saw a large light emanating from what must have been a farmhouse. Someone must be home, we thought, and, once we found a road and knew where we were, we could always phone for a taxi. When we reached the clearing where the farmhouse should have stood, we did feel extraordinarily stupid to find that the light we had seen was, in fact, the light in the sky: a beautiful yellow moon rising into the night.

After that, things turned a bit nasty. Buoyed by a team spirit we tried to remain in good heart, but we had not yet seen the worst the Australian bush had to throw at us. The bush is a serious place: getting lost there is not like losing one's bearings on the fells, and, although none of us would voice it, we knew we were in a proper scrape. We stood on top of a crag at the rim of a huge valley gazing at the stars of the Southern Cross, hoping they would help us to determine our direction (we had neither a map nor a compass), but it was no use at all, as my companions had not been good boy scouts. There definitely was a real place with the lights on at the other side of the valley, but it looked a huge distance away. We headed downhill full of trepidation, as we would have to navigate steep, muddy, loose ground, thick spiky trees and bush, fallen trunks, huge labyrinthine roots and occasional drops over crags. Often, the vegetation was so dense that our feet made no contact with the ground at all. It was scary, desperate and exhausting. Earlier in the day, we had been discussing the early explorers and what it might have been like for them trying to cross the Blue Mountains for the first time.

Now, we were getting a flavour of it. It was at about 11 p.m., after we had been going for five hours, that we reached the bottom of the valley and came to a clearing. There was a small hut with a rain butt and a neat row of upside-down mugs there – civilization! Finally, a drink: we had long since run out of water and, despite the cold, were parched. A good track then led us on through the crisp, sparkling night, and we passed some sleeping livestock. Suddenly, I stopped dead. Having risen, the animals showed themselves to be a group of huge wombats, so big that the ground seemed to shake as they rumbled off. Soon, we were entering a farm garden, and a woman appeared at the door of the farmhouse. "I was just about to leave you a note" was her improbable greeting. After some confused conversation, both parties got the gist of what was being said. Mark's face was a picture when the woman told us we were in Hartley Vale, which is on the other side of the Blue Mountains entirely. It had taken the early explorers years to figure out how to make this crossing. It also transpired that our host had initially mistaken us for the people who were supposed to collect the puppy she had been cuddling inside her coat. Strange goings-on at this time of night, but, after the expected visitors duly arrived, we, along with several other puppies, squeezed into their car and were given a lift to the Comet Inn. It was a charming and historical place with a big fire and a chef who was just about to drive home to the town of Lithgow, in whose main street he deposited us at 1a.m. We were delighted to see that the local takeaway was still open, and, as we waited for a pizza, Mark emptied the climbing kit all over the floor so we could have a sort-out, but with the kit came a heap of dirt. Mortified, Matthew asked for a brush to sweep up. Sometime after 2 a.m., a bemused taxi driver located our car, and we returned to my flat, where a friend had been patiently waiting to have dinner with us. The following evening, I headed to Sydney to catch my flight back to UK. At Manchester Airport, I was glad to see Mandy and Holly the foxhound, and, although I still was not able to feel any sense of homecoming, I returned with a very different concept of what it might mean *to belong*. Experiencing the bush and getting a glimpse of an ancient people connected to their land had awakened my own ancient instinct to connect my soul with a particular corner of the planet. But I felt that this could never be anything more than an unfulfilled longing since I had no roots, no traditions and no deep knowledge of a place in the way that belonged people have. Such things cannot be manufactured they are relationships borne of deep and long commitments.

In Yorkshire, I went straight back to work and finished my training to be a GP. Then we upped sticks to the Lake District and lived in Ennerdale for eight years before moving to Portinscale, just outside the small town of Keswick at the head of Borrowdale.

Borrowdale and its neighbour the Newlands Valley are home to many fine fell races, with the Coledale Race being a perfect, graceful route which starts just a mile or so from our house. The first time I ever ran the Coledale was early on in my fell running. Given that it was a very hot summer evening, I did not bring the proper kit and was disqualified for not having waterproof trousers in my bum bag. I did not mind, as it was a lesson and I really enjoyed the run. The race has now moved from summer to April, and when I ran it recently, the weather was terrible. Sleet and wind were unrelenting. Since I was suffering from a cold, I can only speculate as to why I was daft enough to set off in short leggings. I was probably influenced by my hardier team-mates. The main climb is up Grisedale Pike, and that was okay, but, after the run down to Coledale Hause I started staggering as I approached Eel Crag. Until then, whenever I was racing I always managed to look after myself and to keep warm enough to be safe, but now I was losing it. I could neither think nor stagger, and so I stopped, put on my waterproof trousers, jacket, hat and gloves and ate my emergency jelly babies. After walking up the next hill, I was warm enough to coordinate myself and started running again. The sleet came in worse, and, as we traversed under Causey Pike, I was glad that I knew every inch of the trods over to Barrow, the last little fell. In the whiteout, I could see no one and nothing in front. Wendy, who was behind me, told me afterwards that I was like the Pied Piper, gathering more and more runners on my tail and leading them home. Well, I would, wouldn't I? After all, this was my home. My being has become rooted in these fells because, over the years since returning from Australia, I have given of myself and extended myself here, both alone and alongside special companions. On these hills, I have emptied out my soul to be renewed and refilled. A connection has been formed, and I have found my place in the world. Every morning when the dog and I get beyond the back gate and I look up at Skiddaw, the mountain, while both the same and different each day, is always there and its message is still the same. For a long time, I imagined that I had moved to Portinscale (to the same road on which I had stood, at thirteen, tearfully looking at Skiddaw) simply because I thought it would be a nice place to live – not because of past experiences. But now I wonder. The more that is discovered about the human brain, the more it seems that decisions are made at unconscious levels and that the conscious part just puts a plausible spin on things afterwards, so that we can make sense of ourselves. I could give you a dozen reasons why I think we moved here, but maybe they are not the real ones. It wasn't until long after we had settled in Portinscale that it occurred to me to consciously consider my childhood memory of Derwent Hill and Skiddaw.

Territory is important to animals, and the more human animals there are inhabiting the planet the harder it is for us to feel secure in our own territory, the place where we can roam freely and express ourselves and which we can genuinely get to know. This is why I feel very fortunate indeed to have found just such a place. Only last week, I was out in Borrowdale with Jo and Helen, trotting round the oak woods rich in ancient ecology, and alive with the newness of springtime. Sometimes, I love these places more than the open fells, although it does feel wonderfully free to dance along a ridge top with all the world displayed to gaze on. While the fell tops are wonderfully open, sometimes the fell sides feel barren, shorn like a skinhead by the flocks of Herdwick sheep. It is hard not to sympathise with George Monbiot when he rails against the *sheep-wrecking* of upland Britain in his book *Feral*. Although there is much heritage and tradition surrounding sheep-farming practices, they are neither ecologically justifiable nor economically viable without heavy subsidies. This denuding sterilisation of the land has progressed at an increasing pace since Viking times. In the last decades, it has become more and more evident that the soil is suffering badly, floods are more common and there are fewer flowers. I respect the guardians of our land, but I do feel that practices need to change now and that we need more trees and wildlife so that we can re-establish a balance in our landscape. I would prefer sheep to be much reduced in number and restricted in range so that at least some of the ecosystem, brought into balance, can recover. It is a tradition going back a few centuries to let sheep graze almost everywhere, and it is argued that because the practice is long-established it must have inherent virtue and worth. Yet to doggedly follow accepted custom is the sort of folly that caused the suffragette Emily Davison to die under the King's horse in 1913. Until a hundred years ago it was traditional that women could not vote and it took drastic actions to change the status quo. Tradition does not automatically equate to virtue and sometimes it must be challenged for the greater good. I do support Monbiot's challenge to policy-makers and farmers, to reduce sheep numbers and grow more trees, while, at the same time, believing that the emotionally rooted divisions this proposal has provoked are unhelpful. It would be more constructive if we could all stand back calmly and take a broader view. It is hard, however, to achieve a consensus about how we live on, and use, the land. We all want it to serve our own interests. The sheep themselves do look nice, especially as lambs, and this seems to please city-dwelling visitors. They are a part of the *Lake District brand*. As I write this phrase, I am, thankfully, far enough from Grasmere not to feel the uncomfortable wriggle of Mr Wordsworth in his grave.

Some people seem to feel at home in cities, this being so far removed from my own reality that, at times, I feel as if I belong to a slow-to-evolve branch of our species which is dying out because it cannot adapt. I have noticed that, often, places get defined by how far away they are from other places, this being seen as their selling point. Only five minutes from the bus stop, ten minutes from the station, half an hour to the town centre, etc. Recently in Wasdale, we met a couple who were pleased to tell us they lived in the middle of everything: two hours from North Wales, two hours from the Lakes and two hours from the Peak District. They seemed triumphant about it, but we felt sorry for them, wondering if they knew where they really were at all and if they always just wanted to be somewhere else.

Although going to the gym and running on machines is perhaps a good thing sometimes, and I can see the point in it, I question whether we have lost something fundamental if exercise has become a mechanical event with no other meaning than to improve our physiology. People sometimes think that I run to keep fit or healthy, but that actually is not it at all. I am confident I could be fit and lead a healthy life without something as intense as running. Of course, sport can have many meanings, often very individual and personal, but finding a place on this planet to which I am undeniably connected has been one of the most unexpected benefits of putting on my fell running shoes. Helping me to find a route home has been fell running's greatest gift to me. In some ways, home is more of an emotion than a place, but I feel it most when I am here, under Skiddaw's comforting gaze. To me, this is most succinctly summarised by Billy Bland, who is reported to have said: "Borrowdale is my home. I don't own a square inch of it, but it's all mine!"

A day or two after there had been a trail race around Derwentwater, I came home from a morning run with a bum bag full of litter. Even the race organisers had not bothered to remove all their bits of tape tied to trees to show the route. It may be misplaced snobbery on my part, but it makes me wonder about these kinds of events, which, in spirit, seem to be a little like a road race but in a nice place. Nothing to criticise in that, but a little more care would not have gone amiss. I am sure most trail race organisers are responsible, but long old-fashioned fell races, without any markers to show the way, like the Borrowdale Race itself, feel less like a *use* of the fells and more like a dance with them. The magic lies in the relationship between runner and hill. Like all magic, it cannot be reduced to words and can only be hinted at, but you know when you have been a part of magic weaving. Body and mind completely spellbound in the reckless delight that is flying down Dale Head. It is not possible to hold onto safety and control and to feel like this – it requires a letting go. Rough, tough fell races have taught me about how the letting go of oneself can expand the very definition of what it means to be alive.

It is not up to me to prescribe how others should enjoy this place, my home. After all, it was when I was committing a cultural offence against the indigenous people by going up the rock of Uluru that I first truly understood the nature of the connection between human and earth. I thus have no right whatsoever to make judgements, and, of course, we fell runners have an impact too. Not to mention the fact that many people might say that Herdwicks are, in general, much better-looking than most fell runners.

People sometimes ask, "Don't you miss things racing about, and must you prove yourself in the mountains? Is it not enough to just be with them?" But I enjoy many different ways of being in these places. I am with my guardian, Skiddaw, every day and, each morning, like to stop and look up to see what outfit she has chosen to present to the world: a grey jacket, a feathery hat or a flat cap or, sometimes, a sparkling many-coloured dream-coat or a wispy white shroud. But our relationship is not passive. We have an ongoing collaboration – this mountain and this woman. I have been close to running from Keswick to her summit in under an hour but never quite managed it. My infirmities have prevented any attempts for two long years now, but she is still waiting. My life is the blinking of an eye to a mountain's life, but we live together like intimates, and I still want to give my best run here. If I can do this unwitnessed, it will be my secret gift to my mountain guardian. It is the sort of effort which, for me, comes close to a kind of devotional practice akin to those of the natives of Australia. I used to fill in the religion box on official forms with "Fell Runner" as a joke. Yet actually it is true. And being with, or in, a place can be very fine, as can being up, or on, a mountain, but home is a place to offer your soul to. There is no separation. You belong to it.

Nine

Magic White Hares on a Sunday Morning. The OMM

"Cat, I'm coming in but, just to warn you, I haven't got any clothes on."

Fumbling with frozen hands to open the zip and gain entry to our tiny tent, I did not want to alarm my friend or give her the wrong idea. It was a good thing to have taken off my sodden shorts and top before going in, as getting the inside of the tent wet at this stage would be hell. Cat already had her dry stuff on and had to make herself as small as possible and lie still while I got my dry fleece top and leggings out of a sealed plastic bag and did a contortionist act to wriggle into them inside our modest accommodation. We got into our sleeping bags and set up our tiny stove under the flysheet. A cup of tea, heaven!

Cat and I were doing the Original Mountain Marathon, known as the OMM. That year was the forty-fourth running of the event, which had been going since 1968. Each year, it is staged in a different location in the UK, and, this year, we were in the Highlands of Scotland. It is the only time I have had the privilege of doing a mountain marathon with my friend Cat Evans, although we have had many other adventures together, and Cat, more than any other fellrunner I know, is a mountain woman through and through. I am sure there are other sides to her life, but it is very hard to think of Cat unconnected to the hills.

There are two types of courses on mountain marathons but on all the courses the map is not handed over until the start line so no advanced route planning is possible. There are line courses, where you have to visit a list of checkpoints in a specified order and cannot miss any out, much like in a normal race, apart from each team of two has a different start time to spread people out. There are also score courses, where you have a huge choice of checkpoints worth varying numbers of points, and the goal is simply to get the most points in any order in a specified time. If you go over the time limit points are deducted by the minute. Score courses require much more in the way of strategy and are generally designed to make it almost impossible for any competitor to get all the points, so clever choice of checkpoints is crucial. Although you can get some information from the map about what the terrain might be like, it is impossible to know for certain which parts are good running ground and which are a nightmare. If you get good running underfoot, you can manage several kilometres an hour despite carrying a rucksack with food and camping kit, whereas get onto bad ground and progress can be slowed to a crawling pace. One of the most hated types of ground for mountain marathoners is the type disturbingly referred to as *babies' heads*. These are large floppy tussocks of earth and grass which collapse if you stand on them, but putting your feet between them is very hard work which usually results in getting stuck, falling over, sustaining an ankle injury or any combination thereof.

On this particular OMM, Cat and I were doing the Long Score which meant that we were allowed seven hours on day one and six hours on day two. We arrived at the site of the overnight camp in a hail storm. Putting the tent up and getting warm and dry was urgent, as I was getting bluer by the minute. The weather had been rough all day, but, during the last couple of hours, the wind had strengthened and the rain had got heavier. I had been struggling with an injured ankle and by this stage it was hurting so much that I was reduced to a hobble. Not wanting to risk having the demoralising experience of coming in over the time limit, loosing hard earned points, we cut short our intended route. My ankle had been a problem for a while, but, a few weeks previously, when I was out in Langdale with Geoff Ayers, I had one of those eye-watering, sick-making experiences of putting my foot down a hole and twisting over on it. I pulled myself together, finished the run with Geoff and treated it as a sprain, but the pain had never really gone. The ankle was unstable, and, during the day with Cat, I went over on it a couple of times, although I wasn't worried, as it was not too bad early on. Gradually, however, the pain got worse and worse. We managed to get to the day one finish with time to spare, but, by that stage, I was wincing every time I had to put my right foot down. Working together to get the tent up and sorted required concentration and effort, but we were soon warm and dry and drinking tea. Happy to be in my sleeping bag but worried about my predicament, I silently sipped my comforting brew. I did not know if I should admit that the ankle was feeling really bad. I could now barely walk, so how could I run again tomorrow like this? I was feeling wounded, that horrible weak feeling of needing to crawl into a hole for a while. If it was just me, I could get a lift back to the start the next day and maybe go to A & E to get an x-ray. But it wasn't. Like most mountain marathons the OMM is run in teams of two, and to let Cat down by retiring from the race was my worst nightmare. Cat knew I was hurting but could not help me. She tried to reassure me that pulling out was a definite option and that, if that's what I needed to do, she would much prefer this to my coming to any harm by carrying on. Generally, though, we attempted not to focus on it too much and chatted about other stuff, told each other stories, ate our lovely dehydrated dinner and drank plenty of tea. The OMM is always on the weekend in October when the clocks change, so, while everyone else has an extra hour in a comfortable bed, we are treated to an extra hour in a cramped flimsy tent – often in a gale in the rain. Surprisingly, I did not sleep badly that night and stirred to the atmospheric drone of a bagpiper parading around the field in a kilt in the dark – it was 6 a.m. We were concerned only with looking after ourselves and trying to rest my ankle the night before, and the idea of checking the results on a board at the back of the race official's Land Rover had not featured on our agenda. Our scheduled start for day two was not until after 8 a.m. , and, although there was a kilometre or two up the track to get to the start line, we had loads of time. At least I thought we did. Cat had gone to the stream to get some water for breakfast time tea and in passing she checked the results board. She came rushing back.

"Jules. Quick. Quick. Get the tent down. We are in a chasing start in forty minutes!"

This was not exactly music to my half-awake ears, but, unquestioningly, I immediately rose to the challenge. Cat had discovered we were second in our race and had been put in the *chasing start*. The top few teams from each category are started first, albeit a few minutes apart, so our scheduled later start time no longer applied. Without a second thought, I sprang out of my sleeping bag, got clothes and wet shoes on and stuffed everything in the rucksack. The morning air was blue, my vocabulary having been reduced to a single word beginning with an f. I did, however, make one thing plain.

"Cat. I've got the effing kettle on. I am not effing going anywhere until I have had an effing cup of tea."

Tea downed and sacs packed, we legged it up to the start munching our breakfast on the way. The weather had improved, and, as we got to the line with a couple of minutes to spare, we put this time to use by getting a bit more fluid into us. As we crossed the line, we were handed the map with day two's menu of control points. We then jogged up the track and hunkered down for a few minutes of route planning. The experience of day one gave us some idea of the terrain, and we decided to risk heading out in the direction opposite to the finish, up to some of the bigger hills, hoping to get to some high-scoring controls. The map suggested we would find reasonable tracks there, which was borne out by our making good progress up the first hill. Soon, we were transported from a cold and muddy camp into a beautiful sunny morning. Fading heather and bracken, still rich in colour, were laid out in front of us like an artfully woven carpet displayed in golden sunshine, and, for a couple of hours, we saw hardly anyone. Hares in white coats kept popping up from the vegetation as if out of a hat. I had never seen so many hares: they would leap out and bound off with a speed we could only envy. These were their hills; they were truly at home and probably wondered why runners in pairs kept appearing on their patch. Our navigation flowed and progress was good – no two ways about it: we were having fun. Towards the second half of the allowed six hours, we turned towards home, and the closer we got the more competitors converged on each control point. Energy was diminishing, jelly snakes and Panda Bars were quickly consumed and we were becoming keenly aware we had been a little ambitious and bitten off quite a lot. If we were to make the rest of our intended checkpoints and not be late, we had to speed up. Banking on the fact that the last few kilometres were on a good track, we pushed on, faster and faster. I turned to

Cat and starting chatting, but her riposte made me quickly realise it was not the time for gossip.

"I'm a bit pushed just now; can we talk later?" I guess that was a polite way of telling me to shut up!

As we ran down a track through the woods, the evergreen pines miraculously gave way to a kaleidoscope of splendid autumn Perthshire colours. The trees were putting on a last great show before winter, and, breathless, sweaty and exhausted as we were, their spectacular display was not lost on us as we ran through every shade of red, yellow and gold to get across the line before our time ran out.

"Great run, Cat, thanks."

"Great run, you; by the way, how's your ankle?"

That's funny. It was the first time all day that I even thought about my ankle. As we had won the women's race in the Long Score, we took our time drinking tea and refuelling, enjoying the autumn colours for a while longer, while we hung around for the prize-giving before heading off. I cannot remember how long it took for the pain to come back, but it did. I don't think running the second day made it worse, but it certainly did not cure it either. My scan results showed that a ligament had broken off its moorings, snapping off a piece of bone with it; basically, it was a right mess. After two lots of surgery and a lot of physio, my ankle still hurts a bit now and again and is rather stiffer than the other one, but, most of the time, it's hardly any trouble at all. What is peculiar, though, is that the same ankle, which I could hardly bear to walk on, ran for a wonderful and pain-free six hours the next day. If I had not had such a rude awakening that day, being propelled into action without time to think at all, it may have been a different story.

We tend to think of pain as a response which is in proportion to the strength of the stimulus, but it isn't. Pain happens when a damaged bit of our body sends signals via the nerve endings to the spinal cord and on up into the brain, conveying relevant information. It is one way in which our body can communicate something about what needs to be done to the bit that controls our actions. It was back in the 1960s that doctors Melzack and Wall discovered that the traffic flow of pain signals through nerve fibres into and up the spinal cord and on to the conscious brain is controlled by what they termed *pain gates*. Pain is not a case of a signal being sent at one end and received intact at the other because there are places along the way where the signal can be interfered with and either dumbed down or amplified. The first things that can interfere with the pain signal are other sensations coming in from the same place. Nerves which sense vibration, temperature and touch are thicker than pain-sensing nerves, and, in the case of nerves, a greater diameter equals a faster signal. If these other sensations reach the spinal cord first, they close some of the gates in the spinal cord which would have let pain signals through. This is one reason why we instinctively rub a sore bit better and why TENS machines and massage can be effective painkillers. But it is not just upcoming signals that affect pain gates: the brain itself can send messages down the spinal cord to close the incoming gates to pain. The brain actually sends natural morphine down into the spinal cord in order to do this. This may be one of the mechanisms whereby severe pain can be relieved by an injection of saline delivered as a placebo. In fact, the medical literature cites a World War II army doctor Henry Beecher as the first person to properly document the placebo effect. Having run out of morphine, he used saline to treat severe pain and found it surprisingly effective. Of all medical conditions, pain is most amenable to treatment by placebo because, when the brain has an expectation that the pain will go, it actually makes its own morphine, which closes pain gates down. Being able to block out pain is not just a question of being macho or using mind over matter: it is a real physiological effect, which takes the pain away. There are other chemicals made in our bodies, including ones resembling cannabis, which are involved in these still not fully understood, responses. One of the effects of exercise, such as running, is to stimulate regulated healthy amounts of natural cannabis-like compounds. Our effectiveness at making our own natural painkillers is certainly strongly affected by mood and fatigue. Generally, chronic tiredness or low mood saps the nervous system of resources, and then pain can be felt more keenly. However, if pain signals do get through to the brain when attention and focus are diverted by other strong stimuli, then the pain is less likely to make much impact on consciousness. After all, we are less likely to be disturbed by a burglar in the house if we are so engrossed in something else that we have not realised they have broken in. However, it does mean that the burglar might get away with stealing more which is analogous to the perception of pain, which may have had an important message that went unheeded. Natural painkilling responses can be all well and good to help when you have to carry on functioning for immediate survival, but blocking pain can risk sacrificing the reason why it came on in the first place, i.e. to protect from further injury. Although completing a mountain marathon does not quite qualify as essential for immediate survival, somehow my body must have read the situation as such. Our urgent start had overridden any other demand for my attention, and, by the time we were running, natural opiates, which work like morphine and natural cannaboids, would have been on the go. Then there was, of course, all that happiness, which must also have kept the pain at bay – not to mention the magic white hares and gorgeous autumn trees. How could I have felt any pain? It was unthinkable.

When I first saw the scan report of my ankle, I was a bit shocked and upset. It made for very unpleasant reading, and I did wonder if my fell running days were over. More than that: I was worried about just being able to enjoy the fells and to climb. Thankfully, these fears were fairly short-lived, as there was a big improvement after the first surgery and an even greater one after the second, and the recovery was quick. I tried to retain a modicum of fitness by cycling on a turbo trainer in our garage and doing gym work, but the appeal of such tedious activities does wear thin after a while. Although I was soon up and running, and even hoping to train for other long-distance rounds, I was struggling more and more with back pain, and it seemed that ultra-distance would be an unwise and unrealistic choice. All was not lost, though, and my team-mates drip fed me with the idea of trying the British and English Championships. They are quite clever, these friends of mine: they know better than to give unwelcome advice which will, invariably, be met with bloody-minded attempts to prove them wrong. They sneak ideas in and then make you feel as if you have come up with them yourself. Recently, as part of my work, I went on a course about the principles of psychological influence. It seems that my team-mates need no such course.

Looking back at previous mountain marathons, I can see that it was, in fact, these events that introduced me to running in the hills in the first place. Although, in those days, I did not think of them as competitions, but just a way of having some fun out in great places. While at university, I did an OMM with a friend whom we used to call Suicide Sue or just Suicide for short. Thankfully, her name was nothing to do with her mental state, which was usually very upbeat. Suicide and I learnt to climb together, and, although she was a much better climber, she was somewhat lacking in the general-safety department. Using equipment to protect herself in case of a leader fall wasn't her strongest suit and she often gave us dry mouths watching her bold antics. But her actual climbing was very good so I can gladly report that she is still alive and well! As complete novices, Suicide and I once spent a very wet and windy weekend battling around the Howgills – only to discover later that, owing to the foul conditions, that year's OMM event became a legend among mountain marathons. I must be a very bad person to team up with, as I have had so many different mountain-marathon partners, and only one of them has been patient enough to do more than one event with me. John Byrne and I started doing the OMM for fun and a challenge, and we were not there to compete in any serious sense. A great thing about these events is that a lot of people who take part would not even count themselves as runners, and they mostly walk, and perhaps trot, some sections. There are courses to suit all levels of ability from novice to elite. One year in my junior-doctor days, I remember turning up on a Friday evening for an OMM in the borders of Scotland, and, as John and I were getting our rucksacks ready for the off the next morning, I confessed:

"I am really looking forward to this weekend, John. I just want a complete rest."

He looked at me oddly, probably musing over my sanity, or of lack of it.

"Well, blossom, this is not everyone's idea of a complete rest, but each to their own."

I had spent months running around the wards for eighty to a hundred hours a week. When on call at weekends there was no protected rest whatsoever between Friday morning and Monday teatime, so, to me, this was great. All I had to do was plod, navigate, enjoy the view and enjoy being with John: a perfect, complete rest.

One year, when I was in the midst of my initiation into medicine, Kit mentioned that she had entered the OMM and announced that I was doing it with her. I was a bit bemused, as, at that point, I had not done any running for a very long time. Kit, however, acted as if it was just a perfectly normal thing. She had been an international orienteer in the past and probably just thought nothing of it, being one of those people with a natural fitness which did not seem to rely on constant training. In the end it was really sad that we never got to do that event together because, a week before it, Kit hurt her knee. But, by that stage, I had booked time off and was eager to get out into the hills. As luck would have it, a woman called Katarina had just moved into our house as a lodger. We had met Katarina in Arapiles, a fantastic climbing venue outside Melbourne, where she came from. Katarina, who was a PE teacher, had taken a job at a school near to us for a short time, while she was touring the world. Since PE teachers must be very fit, I thought it was reasonable, when Kit got injured, to enquire of Katarina's plans for the weekend. Having established that she had received no better offers, I roped her into doing the OMM with me. I think I played the event down a bit, but, on Friday, we set off together and set up a tent at the race HQ in the Cheviots of Northumberland. We thought it was a good idea to leave our big tent up, so that, when we got back on Sunday, we could use it to get changed in. But, unfortunately, by the time Sunday came the tent had been destroyed by the wind, and we returned to only broken poles and shredded nylon. On Saturday, though, things started off well enough: we were doing a score class and were picking up plenty of points. But poor Katarina had never been on any hills outside Australia and was not really a runner. I think her specialities were gymnastics and netball. Going over some rough ground, she twisted her knee badly, and it ballooned up. She limped on as I carried both rucksacks, but, dread of dreads, we were late into camp and lost most of the points we had gained. This was a great source of indignation to Katarina, who hobbled around the campsite asking everyone if this was normal, if they had lost any points and if they thought this was fair. Despite my advice to give up she simply refused, so off we went on day two and, this time, managed to keep some points. Katarina is a very beautiful, elegant young woman of Italian lineage, and it was not unusual for her to attract attention. As we went through the finish, a kind marshal, who was dolling out drinks, offered one to my companion with the words:

"Here, love, it's got lemon in it: it will perk you up."

He seemed a little taken aback by Katarina's reply.

"Yeah, mate. I couldn't give an effing rat's arse if it's got gnat's piss in it, cheers."

It was not that my friend had bad manners. She was merely being Australian; translated, her comment would have undoubtedly run: "Thank you so much, my dear chap, I am awfully thirsty".

Katarina's sore knee soon settled down but, unfortunately for her, our house had three floors and her room was at the top. For a couple of weeks, there were some choice Aussie colloquialisms every time she had forgotten to get something she needed from her room and had to force her very sore mountain-marathon legs to make another trip up and down the stairs. She was a great lodger.

When John Byrne and I teamed up, we had lots of fun on OMMs around the country, but by the time I had done the Bob Graham, he had teamed up with another friend. That year the event came to our local venue of Borrowdale and I managed to persuade Sam's husband, Geoff, to join me. Geoff Ayers is an outstanding athlete in his field of triathlon who has done his fair share of fell running in the past, so trotting with me for a couple of days would be no challenge for him. I remember being at their house the day before and Geoff going rummaging in a cupboard after we had checked the forecast. He triumphantly emerged wearing a pair of ski goggles. As it turned out, we needed more than ski goggles to help us to cope the next day. I have been in some winds in wild places such as the Cairngorm Plateau, where it was impossible to make progress by walking, crawling being the only effective method. But I had never been in a situation where even lying on the ground and clinging onto both Mother Earth and my companion would not keep me in situ. Up on our local fells I had become a piece of tumbleweed at the mercy of the elements. Geoff tried his best to keep hold of me as we gradually made downward progress and, around midday, made it through the door of the Swinside Inn, somewhat shaken.

"I don't care if this is a competition, Geoff: there is no way I am going back out there." The place was empty, and we rustled up the chef, who kindly lit the fire and served us some soup, for which we were very grateful.

"Don't worry," the chef reassured us. "Let me tell you, you'll be the first of many." We rang Sam, and, while we were waiting for her to drive over and rescue us, endless pairs of half-shredded runners stumbled in vowing they could not go on. What happened over the next few hours is the stuff of legend. Geoff and I were feeling relieved: we had been fed, had put our dry clothes on and got into Sam's warm car to go back round to race HQ and officially retire from the race. By this time the road was flooded, so we could make only so much progress in the car. We got out and waded waist deep towards the race officials' office in a barn when a Land Rover came towards us pushing a huge wave of water, which lifted me off my feet in an almighty swell. "Oh, it's a tsunami," Geoff laughed. So much for dry clothes. And, when we got to the HQ to hand in our dibber, they were rather surprised we had not realised the race had been called off very shortly after it began.

Even after heavy rain Sourmilk Ghyll above Seathwaite is usually just a couple of metres wide but, as we looked up, the torrent now resembled Niagara Falls, tons and tons of raging, foaming water powering over the fell into the valley. I had never seen anything like this before, but it was so powerful and, in its way, so astoundingly beautiful that I felt awed rather than frightened. "Wow!" – I stared open mouthed, finding it hard to take in. This was our Borrowdale yet not in my wildest dreams had I ever imagined it could be like this. Sam's driving over Honister Pass to get us all home was impressive and fearless. My sense of unreality persisted as a fast flow of water tumbled huge boulders down the road. We picked up waifs and strays we recognised along the roadside and took them back to our place for the night but were unable to locate John Byrne and his running partner. It turned out they were safe, having spent a wet night in John's car. They recovered, but I don't think the car was ever quite the same again. Back at home in Ennerdale, we were curled up by the fire, but the phone kept ringing, as word was out about what had happened on this year's OMM. One of my friends wisely advised me to ring my mother, as the OMM was the main story on that night's BBC News at Ten. I was not pleased that we made news on national TV. At the time, Mandy was in Kathmandu and rang up Sam to see if Geoff and I were okay, as the story had now made international headlines. True to form, bulletins screamed: "Hundreds of runners lost without trace", which was on a par with the level of accuracy one often finds in the press. In actual fact, everyone was sheltered and safe.

You never know what you are going to get when you sign up for an OMM: a complete rest or a very wild time. I remember one occasion in Wales when John and I had been given an early start time on day one and so were among the first competitors to get into camp. It was a warm sunny afternoon, and we had the pick of the pitches, so we set up in the best spot and spent the afternoon drinking tea, chatting with the incoming folk and sunbathing. At other times, however, the weather would be so bad that it was a major achievement to keep the tent up for the night and get to the day two start with food inside us and dry clothes on.

There are now quite a number of other mountain marathons besides the OMM, all around the country and at different times of year. One year, I persuaded Mandy, who is a devout non-runner, to take part with me in a two-day event in the Howgills. She enjoyed the tactics and navigation involved in the score event, but her feet suffered, as she was in borrowed shoes. Looking back now she does say it was fun and she would like to do another one in better footwear. That is the thing about these marathons – there is something for everyone. Lean and keen racing snakes cut off labels to save weight and pare down their kit to the barest possible minimum, while others have fun time plodding or trotting along while carrying warm sleeping bags, Thermorests, *real* food and hip flasks. Comparing one of these mountain marathons to something like a road marathon in a city is impossible. While they are both running competitions, and both have the word marathon in the title, that's where any similarity ends. It is interesting that, when you think about the skills and fitness required to actually win the OMM, it does seem a lot more impressive than running along a road. I do not mean to belittle road runners, as it does take extraordinary talent and dedication to run that fast. And each type of event has very different rewards. The prize money for first place in the London marathon is around fifty-five thousand dollars, whereas, if you are astonishingly good in the OMM, you might win some shoes and a nice jacket. But none of us mountain-marathon runners would have it any other way. True, there are sponsored athletes on the fell and in mountain running, but none of them will ever make much from it, and none of them will ever be afforded the type of support available to professional athletes on the road. Yet our rewards cannot be accounted for like that. Nowhere is it more evident that fell running is not a sport that can be reduced to numbers and rankings than on the overnight camp on an OMM at the end of October. People huddled together in pairs in tiny tents, with their best friend, wife, husband, lodger, son, daughter or team-mate. Hundreds of participants, cheek by jowl in some remote unlikely field. Some swear when others trip over their tent guys in the dark, some just burst out laughing at friends falling over in thick mud and everyone thinks it's great to be woken up by a bagpiper at 6 a.m. – be there wind, rain, frost or moonlight. It is impossible to put any metric on this type of fun which is hard to truly describe. You just have to be there to understand it.

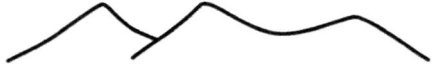

Ten

A Fate Worse Than Death

It was the sort of day that made me feel nervous about taking off my thermal and windproof. The prospect of running in a vest wasn't inviting. Jo Gillyon, Helen Winskill and I were warming up at the start of Pendle Hill Race. Warming was definitely required, as it was the first week in April, cold, windy, grey and damp. Warming up for an important race can be a tricky time, and Jo could sense I was not at my best.

"You'll be okay, love," she encouraged me, "anyway, what's the worst that can happen?"

I hesitated, my demeanour becoming even more grave. Suspecting that an injection of humour might help, Jo persisted: "Well, I suppose you could die."

To which I responded immediately: "Oh no, dying would not be the worst thing: I would not be worried about dying – I am worried about having a crap race!"

Luckily, Helen appeared and responded to Jo's request: "For God's sake, you try and talk some sense into her."

When I turned fifty, I decided to give the English and British Fell Championships a go, as, in theory, being at the young end of a new age group maximises one's chances. It was not my first choice, as I had been harbouring ambitions to do longer challenges, and distance had always been my strength, but my back seemed unable to cooperate in those schemes. But the champs were not too shabby as a second-best goal to focus on. The first race in the English series at Pendle was held a week before my fiftieth birthday, so, although the result could not count in my championship effort, we thought it would be a good idea for me to do it for practice. There are six races in the English series, with the best four performances to count. Even though this would not be one of my counters, I was still very nervous since it was a test of how I was likely to fare against the same competitors after my birthday. All I could think of was how unfit I was. This was not because of general moral decrepitude or laziness on my part but was the result of being injured and having surgery on my right ankle a few weeks previously. However, while I was warming up for the race, my brain had equated this situation to a feeling of being out of place and not deserving to compete with these, much better, athletes. What do you think you are doing here? nagged the voice inside. You are just going to make a fool of yourself. Helen tried talking some sense into me as we did a few last drills before lining up.

"You can only do your best and think about yourself. You cannot have any effect on what anybody else can do. Just run your race, enjoy it!"

Then, it was time to cut the chat, and off we went. I struggled the whole way. I was tense, and neither my breathing nor my stride flowed, and I had tight feeling in my guts. I managed to keep with Helen and Jo on the lung-busting ascent straight up the front of Pendle Hill, so steep we had to, at times, use hands on the slope in front of us. They encouraged me on, "Go on, Jules", but I don't think I even managed a grunt in reply. On the downhill, I tried not to let Helen get past me but felt wobbly and could not run in a good line or get anything to flow. Gasping across the finish fields with my legs feeling wooden, I could see plenty of my age-group competitors just ahead but trailed in behind. And really – what was it about a short fell race in Lancashire that could be scarier than dying? I was unsure until I really thought about it.

The prospect of my racing in a national competition and having the cheek to think I could try to win a medal was a full-frontal assault on my personal stories. The stories which I had come to believe so powerfully. The ways I had learnt to make sense of my world. At Pendle, there was a battleground inside me. Deeply engrained and long-held negative scripts were making a bid to be heard and acted out, which is why I had felt so dreadful. I fooled myself into thinking that these dragons of self-disgust had been slain long ago, and, afterwards, as my chat with Jo and Helen played through my mind, I doubted if I had the bravery to face them again.

We can know the world in different ways: through our own direct experiences, through education, i.e. by accessing the common body of humanity's amazing and ever-growing knowledge, and through stories. Narratives give us the context, the sense, the meaning. Cultural meanings are perpetuated through stories like the ones in the Bible or the Koran, or even those in the Daily Mail or on EastEnders. Celebrities shape our modern culture through the stories they enact on screen or tell in songs. Children love stories and easily learn when, transfixed and entranced, they are under the spell of a good tale. Politicians are professional storytellers, and so are marketing experts. When driving, I sometimes start listening to a radio play and if the journey finishes before the story, I have to sit in the car and wait to hear the end. Our brains just hate not knowing the end of a story, and it is thought that this may have something to do with why we dream. If, in the day, we experience various emotional states which we do not act on, there is unfinished mental business, and dreams are a way of finishing off the emotional stories. Things only ever make sense if we can place them within a coherent story.

Stories, often rich in emotions, give meaning to our lives, and, with the power of stories in human psyche being paramount, logical reasoning is often up against it. Our emotional brain evolved long before our clever deductive thinking bits, and so belief is often a much more powerful force than reason. This, along with the fact that we have an instinctive tendency towards pessimism, can have unfortunate consequences. Anything that has a vague whiff of being a threat tends to be instinctively exaggerated, a tendency which journalists love to exploit. Of course, the world is full of real threats, and, with humans having evolved in a generally risky environment, wariness makes sense as a survival tactic. It's all too easy to combine natural wariness with emotionally charged beliefs to produce some extremely destructive stories about ourselves. At Pendle, I was still working off an old version of my personal script. No matter that I had been recovering from an injury and that there were athletes there with more talent and experience and more training behind them. Such reasonable acknowledgments did not gain any air space in my brain that day. I was simply working off the old mantra of "I'm rubbish". It had played through my head so many hundreds of thousands of times that it was automatic or, what psychologists would call, conditioned.

It is not possible to run in a national championship with the mindset of "I want to win but I am rubbish". I could say one of these things but not both, as they were two mutually exclusive versions of reality, and only one story could be chosen. It's odd, really, that the challenge to let go of a story and believe in a different and, indeed, better one was so painful. But that's how we humans are, as history testifies that we do not give up our stories and beliefs easily – not even when they stop being useful or real. There are enough armed conflicts in our modern world to suggest that we still need to make progress in this area. When I was a child growing up with violence, neglect and abuse, I did not think – I don't deserve this. It is happening because my parents are in a mess. I witnessed my mother's secret suffering as my father, who was himself tortured by his own brutal child-hood, drank himself into anger and played out his frustration, sexually and violently. When my time came, I was already a terrified child, easy prey for my grandmother's new husband. I lost my virginity at age eleven. I may have been twelve, the exact date is not the thing I remember most and, despite my resilience, I still feel sickened by it. Just as any child would, I thought, this is bad stuff because *I am bad*. This belief in my own *badness* became a strong running theme in my life script. At the time, it made sense. Complete sense. In fact, it was the only conclusion my childhood self could come to. Even though most of us are biologically predisposed to be a little threatened by the world and therefore wary, we also tend to trust the significant adults in our early lives. And trusting them meant I believed that I deserved what I got.

Here I was at Pendle, almost fifty and still not grown up. I had still not escaped the grip of the powerful bad-child story. I was still not really able to believe a new story and was still allowing myself to be wasted on the negative narrative, succumbing to the feeling that all my tomorrows must be defined by my yesterdays. All sports are a kind of game, and I could not even play at allowing myself to truly flourish. But therein was an opportunity, a chance. If I could play at being good at something, maybe it would help. Or should I content myself with some easy local races and nice outings with the dog. Why put myself through this if I was not going to enjoy it? Deep down, I knew there was a reason.

In sport, as in any arena of human endeavour which requires a real effort, the role of scripts is of paramount importance. We can only truly engage in an activity which takes enormous effort if, in our minds, there is a sense in it, a plausible story. Scripts and stories can be used, consciously or otherwise, to help or to sabotage our effort. If they are unconscious, the danger is that they start to undermine us, so being conscious of our scripts can avoid this pitfall. Some unhelpful scripts that fell runners might play through their minds are:

"I am crap on rough ground, so I am dreading the descent,"

"I hate the start: I cannot stand all that pressure,"

"Jo Bloggs is a much better climber than me; I bet he burns me off on the first hill and it will be hell to try and catch him."

My Pendle scripts were familiar:

"You know you are rubbish. You will never be able to compete with these people. They are proper runners,"

"Your team will be ashamed of you,"

"You cannot do this; you do not deserve to be here. You're just rubbish."

When it came to racing on the fells, there were other, more adult, themes which supported my lack of self-respect. I was very shy of admitting to being competitive and harboured a general feeling that a competitive streak is an uncivilised sort of trait. A personal feeling that trying to win things is not really what I am about in life. And perhaps a cultural thing that, for a middle-aged English woman, pursuits such as flower arranging or knitting were perhaps more suitable than competing in fell races. It was not until I really understood what racing was doing to me that I became comfortable with my dirty little competitive secret. One of the reasons why racing has been such an efficacious therapy for me is that it has forced me to rewrite many of the stories and beliefs that have held me back.

But, on that grey morning in Lancashire, the emotions I was experiencing, reminding me that I was *rubbish*, were excruciating, and I knew that death did not have to be excruciating. In any case, physical pain is a lot easier to handle than this sort of emotional torture. After my birthday, there were five more races in the English Championship. Five races the running of which re-programmed my mind. Never again would I, or will I, experience the torture of *rubbish-hood*. The destructive scripts I had learnt as a child and young adult were subdued by the many good things I experienced in my thirties and forties, but, although their volume was subsequently turned down so much that they were often inaudible, I was never in a situation where they had been wiped off the tape altogether. Racing was akin to the enlightenment of science trying to expose truth. Racing forced me to confront some personal lies, some faulty but deeply conditioned beliefs. At last, I had something which had the strength to wrestle me into letting to let go of my *I'm rubbish* story. Five more races. Could I do them, would I cope?

Although the crunch point came at Pendle, in terms of my inner battles it had taken the forces for change within me a while to marshal their resources. I had done the Bob Graham when I was forty-two. Pendle was just before my fiftieth birthday. For some of the intervening years, I was not able to race or run as much as I would have liked, being held back partly by physical problems related to my spine and partly just by being too busy in, and tired from, work. But, in those years overall, I did do a fair bit of fell running and a respectable amount of racing, albeit inconsistently. I even won a silver medal in the English Championships in the veteran forty-five age group, which was a tremendous boost to my confidence. That silver was in 2011, and I am thankful for the Fell Running Association's on-line records because I could not clearly remember the races in the 2011 championships. How odd: I had expected that, when I looked those records up, the memories would come flooding back, but no. I vaguely remember the Duddon Race being on a nice day and being pleased with my time at three hours and fifty-four minutes, over two hours faster than my first attempt. I remember going to Shropshire for the first time and the brutal, steep running of the Long Mynd, where the course had a profile like an unrelenting roller coaster. I can also recall it being a misty day on the Loughrigg Silverhow Race from Ambleside and a competitor from one of the Yorkshire teams calling over to me for advice on the line to take and me yelling back, "Head straight for that sheep." Well, it was the only visible landmark.

I was enjoying myself fell running, and, although these races were not making indelible impressions on me, I think they were slowly building me up. I felt that, to some extent, I was getting the hang of this sport, but, on the whole, I often felt rather outclassed, as there were many much faster women out there than me. It did not matter: I just loved doing it, and I could feel it strengthening me: mind, body and spirit. There have been races I did not enjoy, but fewer than one hand's worth. Sometimes I did well, at other times not, but almost every time I came home from a race I had something to be pleased about. The plain and simple truth is that most of the time it just felt good to be doing it. There is no record of me in the 2012 or 2013 championships – what was I doing? I think I was probably struggling and did not have the resources to look after my physical problems and keep myself well enough to race. The problem in my back means my biomechanics are appalling, and sustained periods of running require huge amounts of preparatory work, such as stretching and strengthening, etc. I did not have the time, energy or know-how to keep my wonky body on the go.

When, occasionally, I did do well in races during my forties, I found it very pleasing, but I often found a slight mismatch between what I wanted and what I thought I was capable of. It's possible to interpret these feelings in different ways. Maybe I am not as good as I would like to be and so must always be a bit disappointed about that, as well as being a bit envious of those who are good runners. It would be nice to be good, but I needed to accept that I was mediocre. I must admit that this is how I felt now and then – until I understood my feelings a bit better and realised that this constantly wanting to improve does not need to be a source of disappointment. We all have it, this desire and need to extend ourselves. That's why, if life gets too comfortable, it can start to feel boring or even meaningless. Feeling pleased on the whole but not quite as good as one would like is actually the best place in the world to be. When then would I be satisfied? After a good race, I usually feel satisfied for a few days. But if you ask me at any one moment if I am satisfied with my running, the answer is never ... and always.

One of the races from this phase of my running which really does stick in my mind was the Noon Stone. It was the first race in the English Championship series of 2010, and I can remember it as if it were yesterday. Mandy and I were on our way to a climbing holiday in Glencoe. We went via the race in our own car so that we could get up to Scotland and meet up with our climbing friends straight afterwards. Mandy was pleased that the weather was cold, which boded well for ice climbing. When we got to the Calder Valley in West Yorkshire, I was mighty glad I had been to look round the course beforehand. It was a misty day, and there was a long featureless section across a boggy moor in the middle of the route. We started off up the first grind, quickly followed, like a bad joke, by a descent down the same hillside, which meant another big climb up past Stoodley Pike Folly, slippery and steep. The next couple of miles to Withen's Clough Reservoir were rough and tussocky in parts but not too bad. As we got onto the bleak bit, it started snowing. Not everyone's idea of fun, this. There was a biting headwind and the ground was not quite frozen enough to prevent my feet from breaking the surface and sinking into the sapping icy bog. At one point, I went in deep, and, as I pulled and heaved to free my legs, I felt a sucking from under me and only seemed to sink in deeper. Becoming frantic, I yelled at the next man who passed me, "Get me out, get me out!" Fell running is a friendly sport, thank God. Sometimes, helping each other is more than a matter of courtesy – our lives can depend on it. My rescuer had me out with one big tug, and we resumed the job in hand of getting over the moor against the wind and sleet. I was somewhat numbed, but, after what seemed like several hours but was probably about thirty minutes, the moor ended. The descent back to Mankinholes was down a path which, in this weather, had become a runnel of large unstable rocks on a mud slide. Excitement rose within me, as I could see some of the runners in my age group easily within my reach, and, being relatively good at downhill, I was out to catch them. It was at this point that I realised I was missing something crucial, namely a large portion of the left side of my visual field. I knew what was happening and was damned annoyed. The cold had sparked off the visual aura I occasionally get as a form of migraine. But I must have been truly determined, as I just kept going and, for the last few hundred metres, trusted to luck that I was not going to seriously hurt myself. Having to rely only on the eyes in my feet did slow me down a bit, and I came fourth in my age group. I remember feeling very sick and faint sitting by the drystone wall in the lane after the finish, where Mandy came to rescue me and scoop me up to go off on our holiday. I presented her with the nice blue and yellow buff all the competitors had received as a memento. Not my greatest race in terms of performance, and yet I felt pleased with myself for coping and have never forgotten it. Sometimes it is the experience, the amount and depth of what is put in and committed rather than the winning or losing, that makes a treasured memory.

A few months after the Noon Stone, Mandy and I were in Nepal with our friend Martha Evans. The three of us were crossing a very unfrequented high pass in the Kanchenjunga massif. No one had been over the pass for at least a couple of years, so the best route up the boulder-strewn glacier and snowfield was unclear. Our two Nepalese companions were to accompany us to the top and carry the lion's share of our luggage before leaving us to negotiate the glacier down the other side by ourselves. Progress was hard-won, but we were rewarded with vistas on a massive scale and delighted to see some snow-leopard prints in the snow. Half way up, our two porters complained of headaches and refused to carry on. It was evident that Jongdella and his friend were struggling. The situation had not been helped by me buying a yak-wool rug in Ghunsa, which added another three kilos on the pack. They agreed they could carry on if given more money, but it was when Jongdella secured his real heart's desire, Mandy's Noon Stone buff, that he instantly became like a spring chicken again. I hope you are still healthy and laughing, Jongdella, and still wearing the Noon Stone buff. I often think of you and smile on the many occasions I make the same mistake of taking something at face value and not understanding that one thing can mean something else, and different things, to different people. Of course, this is a line of reflection which is close to my heart, as it represents the essence of what has been referred to as the *art of medicine*. A Sherpa with a headache did not want a painkiller or a drink, or even more money: he wanted a Noon Stone buff.

Logically, I knew that my belief in my being rubbish was also a reflection of something different – a misinterpretation of events which my childhood brain could not grasp in any other way. This is obvious to the reasoning mind, but these patterns become hardwired, and changing our story requires a lot more than insight: it requires the lived experience of a new reality. The modus operandi of the human brain is to match current experience to known patterns. At every moment of our lives, we are interpreting things in the light of what we can recognise, of what has gone before. The way in which we experience each moment is, in part, defined by all the moments which have gone before. Showing up in a big race being unfit and not ready made me feel nervous, intimidated, scared. These were feelings I knew well. Being shut down by fear was an old and familiar sensation to which I automatically and subconsciously associated with the my old familiar interpretation – I was rubbish. What had happened to all that strength and confidence that racing had been building in me? Clearly, they were more fragile than I had imagined; I did not like this feeling, and no amount of thinking about it would help. It would take action to change things. Another big hero of mine is the swimmer Diana Nyad, the only person to swim from Cuba to Florida, which she did at age sixty-four. Her TED Talk, *Find a Way*, is unmissable. Diana is fond of quoting Socrates, "To be is to do". What I had to do after Pendle was five more English Championship races. What I had to do was weave a new thread into my story and weave it so tightly that it would change the fabric of my being. Five more races. I am sure that people have spent thousands of pounds and years in therapy and not gained as much benefit as I did from those five races. There's both a lump in my throat and a smile on my face when I remember them.

Eleven
A Change of Mind

Big birthdays can sometimes provoke a little evaluation and reflection, taking stock of one's life so far. In the back of my mind, I knew that, if I could not stop making excuses and get on with racing that summer, it would be a source of deep regret. Making choices which we know we will regret in the future is just stupid, and so, being fifty, I thought it about time that I should try to make a serious attempt at growing up.

Race 1

The next race in the 2014 English Championships after my gloom at Pendle was Coniston in early May. Coniston is quite a tough race, steep going right from the off and unrelenting all the way up to Wetherlam summit. After that, there is a lot of good running over Swirl How and up to Coniston Old Man, where the last few hundred metres to the summit are like running up a sloping playing field. There is the thinnest margin of grass and, in places, just bare earth where Herdwicks have grazed and humans have trodden the ground to an almost lifeless plateau. While this part of the fell is incredibly smooth, it's still uphill and far enough into the race to struggle with a fast pace. Just as my energy was waning, I could see an orange vest a couple of hundred metres or so in front. That must be the Bowland runner I was battling with up Wetherlam, and, like a red rag to a bull, her bright orange vest set an alarm off in my thoughts. I needed to beat this woman – she is in my age group. Tired legs and laboured breathing were relegated down the list of important information, and my focus became the chase. I got closer and closer and, soon, overtook her. Then, glancing sideways, I realised that this was not my rival: it was someone else, a man from the same club. My eyesight is not my best asset, but the bright orange had worked a treat, and I approached the summit with some confidence. Descending Coniston Old Man efficiently is an art form, but I had it wired, having spent a happy few hours, one evening a couple of weeks previously, running up and down it by all available routes and finally mastering the speediest line. That's not to say it's easy even when you do know every turn and trod: there is a lot of concentration required to get the feet to land safely without having a braking effect and to take off high enough not to trip over the loose scree and boulders which have been carelessly left strewn over the mountainside. Does nobody in fell racing really care about health and safety? Committing to a descent like this is a bit like climbing. Tensing up by trying to keep control is no good. It's not a case of throwing oneself at it either. It is a case of using the bodies skill acquired through experience. A wonderful coexistence of relaxation and concentration. Soon, I was off the hill, and, after a quick run down the track and a steep lane, I reached the finish field. Thanks to being prepared and having a good descent, not to mention the motivating orange vest, I had had a good run, coming third in my age group. I wondered if I could stay that high up in the reckoning by the end of the season.

Race 2

Ennerdale was next. The very word made me excited, as I remembered my best ever race in 2008, when I ran the Ennerdale off the back of marathon training and had a turn of speed. This time, though, I knew I did not have that kind of fitness. Sometimes, I prefer to compete in unfamiliar races, as then there is no pattern or expectation to match up to. Having had a bad race makes it hard to go back but does provide an incentive to put things right. Having had a good race, on the other hand, can give confidence but does exert pressure to measure up. But this was Ennerdale, my special place: what could go wrong? Friends of mine were pleased that I had started racing again after a couple of years struggling with back pain and not being up to much. John Byrne said he would see me at Scarth Gap, Alison Scott said she might be having a walk up to Green Gable, and my friends Annemieke and Sarah said they would be going on an outing up Haycock. It was a wild day with thunderstorms forecast, and, at Ennerdale Scout Centre, I was going through endless deliberations about what to wear and became worried about the state of my shoes. In races, I love to wear old-fashioned Walsh shoes because they are the only ones which I trust on rough ground and which do not hurt my feet. Walshs are fantastic but not very hardwearing. I had resurrected this pair from our garage for the Coniston Race, but the sole was beginning to peel off. This was no time to skimp, and, in a rare fit of eager shopping, I got a new pair from the Pete Bland mobile shop, declining the bag as I was keeping them on. Next came an announcement: because of the weather, the route was being altered and would involve a detour down to Crummock Water and missing out some of the tops, as marshals would not be safe in these conditions. I was unable to get phone reception to convey this to my friends who had already set out to get to our various intended rendezvous. But I could not worry: we were about to start. This is a runner's race I thought to myself. Remember all that flat running you have done in the past; you can make the most it. Fell runners have different strengths: rough stuff, steep stuff, intimidating descents, but none of these is my strength. Oddly, my forte is pace on easily runnable sections: I am really built for the road – if only I loved it. Knowing that the diversions would involve easy gradients on good paths my confidence was growing by the minute. When we started, I ran towards John like a dog to its master, covering the miles of straightforward ground up to Scarth Gap with a determined and focused effort. After that, it was more like a fell race again, so my legs had a shock adjusting to the slower, rougher ground. Having realised the route had been diverted, Alison came down to the valley head to encourage me on. Thunder rumbled, lightning buzzed, rain came down, and the wind got up. I was glad we were not running all the summits. As I was coming down the last rough fell, the weather got even worse, and I was happy to get back to the valley path past Black Sail Youth Hostel. Joss Naylor was there with a "Well done, lass", and John was waiting with more food and drink. My mind wanted me to fly and burn up the next four miles down the forest track, but my legs were not used to the pace: it was a long time since that marathon training. Before the bridge over the River Liza, I was hurting so badly I had to slow down to a walking pace. Not able to capitalise at all on the easy running, I was fuming inside. This is a flat track: come on, run; this is what you are good at. I knew my rivals were behind me but was sure they would appear any minute now. Almost in tears with the cramp in my adductor and back muscles, I crouched down on the trail. Gingerly, I lay there in the rain trying to gently stretch. Minutes went by, the sound of running feet approached, and a couple of men trotted past asking if I was alright. Lying down in a race must not have looked very convincing but I assured them I was fine, trying desperately to believe myself. As more minutes passed I eased myself back to walking, and still no women had overtaken me. Gently jogging again, I tried drinking more and started getting a proper running stride back – not fast but running nevertheless. Trying to run along the south side of Ennerdale lake with leg cramps is a bad, bad joke. It is like something out of that old TV show *It's a Knock-out*, only the obstacles are not soft foamy things – they are slippery, unstable boulders that can hurt. Staying upright was almost too big a challenge, and, sometimes, I leant down and slithered along, having to talk to myself out loud just to keep from curling up in pain. Eventually comes a bit under Anglers Crag, where a wrong foot placement would mean a slip off the edge akin to that from a high board and an early bath in the lake several metres below. Then, it's an easy few hundred metres back to the Scout Centre. After the finish, I cried in pain, hurting from my waist to my feet. Knowing it would only get worse if I did not sort myself out, I pushed myself to get changed and dry. At prize-giving, when Joss called me out as the first vet 50 woman, I was unable to stand up straight but did manage a shuffle to the front for a handshake and another special "Well done lass". I did not know whether I should be worried or pleased, but I had to drive myself back to Keswick, and that was quite enough to think about at that moment. Until I remembered Annemieke and Sarah. Oh dear. I found out later that, after waiting through the thunderstorms in their group shelter at Haycock for hours until mildly hypothermic, they had come home. Finally, when I got to tell them the result, I started to feel pleased. It was my first age-group win in a championship race.

Race 3

On another steamy July morning, we arrived for the Kentmere Race under dramatically rumbling skies. This time Mandy and our young trail hound, Moss, and lots of Keswick runners, were out for the day with assorted cakes and picnics. Kentmere is another demanding but beautiful horseshoe race, which I had done before, the last time in a dreadful heatwave. A storm was gathering as I ran up onto High Street via a line of undulating summits, and it was only a matter of time until the downpour started. And when it came, it really came. Thunder, lightning, hailstones – the works. With the return via Kentmere Pike, the run from the last hill to the finish line is quite a way, but my legs were wheeling down the final descent, and the crackling in the atmosphere and the taste of electricity on my lips only added to my excitement. The last couple of miles through lanes and fields seems to go on and on. I could hardly see through the torrential downpour, and, finding myself with no other runners nearby, I had to race myself to keep up any pace. As thunder clapped, I crossed the line, wetter than wet. When I got my breath back, I was puzzled to see Gill Myers, last year's vet 50 champion and a much faster runner than me. I would have expected that she would be finished and changed by now. I handed her my print-out of splits and the final time, as, with no glasses, I could not read it myself.

"Oh sorry, Julie."

"What do you mean sorry? Did you beat me by ages?"

"Twelve seconds."

Gill is the best of competitors, and I think a part of her was genuinely sorry.

"My God. Don't be sorry, well done."

We gave each other a very wet hug and went off for replenishment, but I was flabbergasted. I could not understand how Gill could have been so close in front without me seeing her. Then again, it was in a hailing thunderstorm, and my vision is bad even on a clear day. Besides, Wharfedale, her team, wear white vests, which don't attract attention as much as bright colours. Since Mandy was not back from Kentmere Pike, where she had been waiting to cheer me on, I sat in someone else's car as various delicious homemade cakes were passed round. Everyone had things to say, offered post-race reflections and gave satisfied sighs, but I could only muster two words: "Twelve seconds". The margin was too painfully small to accept. I like and respect Gill a lot, and I had been surprised to beat her at Ennerdale, but now the gauntlet was down. She is certainly faster than I am, but, sometimes in long races I can dig in and come through. Can somebody please arrange to add a mile onto the Kentmere in future?

Race 4

The Sedbergh Hills Race was the August fixture, and I had more than one score to settle. The previous time I raced the Sedbergh Hills, I let myself down. I can navigate in bad visibility and knew the route anyway, but, enveloped in thick mist, I followed some other experienced runners in the heat of the moment, feeling confident they would have it wired. A big embarrassed group of us ended up in the wrong valley with a huge rough climb over steep scree to regain the race route. After the finish line, I threw my bum bag down in disgust: how could I have been so stupid! Not only had I made the disgraceful error of following others instead of my own judgement, but now I was having a paddy about it. Redemption was called for: I must give a better account of myself this time. The warm-up at Sedbergh is on a football field, and, as I started doing a few strides, my heart began pounding in my chest. Wondering what was going on, I started having memories of my final medical exams. My body had registered a reality that my thoughts had not dared to dwell on. If I could win, as I had at Ennerdale, then I was in with a chance of championship. A medal would have been very pleasing, but winning it:

that was another thing altogether. I went to the loo, where I recalled my final exams: despite being nervous, I had passed with good marks. I had words with myself and used my breathing to calm my adrenalin. Just be calm, try to concentrate and get on with it. Running off into the hills on that showery, blustery day, I did get on with it, and fourteen miles and six thousand feet later I cruised in, with no mistakes: the first old woman. Now things got interesting.

Race 5

On a sunny mid-September morning, Mandy and I drove to the Hodder Valley Show in the Trough of Bowland, which, although it is not very far from Cumbria, is a place I had never been to. Good then to have the last race on new turf, but what was not good was that it was a very short race, and short races are very much my weakness. There was no way I could beat Gill over four miles, but actually I knew that I did not need to. The way things stood, I just needed to come second in this race, and I would still win the championship overall. My team-mate Lyn Thompson had also come along to gee me up as much as anything else. Lyn, a many times champion herself, would not be expecting anything but my best effort. I find it desperately hard to get into a fast pace quickly, and, on the first hill, Lyn, who was right behind me, sounded slightly incredulous about my sedate start: "Come on, Julie, get moving". I did my utmost, and, three miles in and with just one last short rise and a final descent, I knew that I was fourth in my age group. I was running as fast as I could, but I just was not good over this distance. As we hit the final rise, I faced myself and simply thought: Well, the only thing you can do is run faster. At that moment, in which I genuinely perceived that I was already giving a hundred percent, I found another gear. I questioned myself frankly: Are you sure that is all you've got; just run faster, can you? As soon as I found I could make myself run faster, it seemed almost easy. It was simply a choice, and I was calling the shots. The effort and the discomfort became irrelevant, and I just ran faster and, with a certainty I had never had before, overtook all the others except Gill. This was the moment when I became able to create a new story, when today became a blank page which it was within my power to write on. Reaching the last top in second place, I knew I was the best descender so I would hold on. Pushing on across the finish fields and down the gravel track to the line I did not dare to look back. After the finish, we all cruised round the show, being entertained by sheep-shearing contests and flower arrangements, with one of my rivals, Rowena of the orange Bowland vest, buying me a tea and cake to celebrate.

On the way home I rang my friend Ed Gamble. I am sure that he would not have sounded prouder if I had won the Nobel Prize for Medicine. "That's brilliant, Jules: you are an English Champion!" I remember a part of the journey home, with Mandy driving and me chatting to Ed. I remember it like a movie: the sturdy drystone walls along the quiet windy road, the powder blue sky with fluffy white clouds, the aching in my legs and the warmth in my soul. I knew that this was only significant in my tiny little personal world, but, at the same time, I knew it was significant for me. I understood the reason why I had not contented myself with local races and nice outings with the dog. In his wonderful book *Man's Search for Meaning*, the holocaust survivor Victor Frankl, in a completely different context, offers the perfect words: "Between stimulus and response there is a space. In that space is our power to choose our response. In our response lies our growth and our freedom." I cannot, by sheer effort of will, decide to become Paula Radcliffe or even beat my friend Gill Myers in a short fell race. But what I *can* do is to try to consciously inhabit the space where I choose my responses. It cannot always be possible to choose to run faster, but it is possible to decide to try.

All summer during this English Championship series, there had been a sub-plot, and that was the British champs, in which there is a race in each country: England, Scotland, Wales and Northern Ireland. The best three performances count. One race always counts for both English and British, and that was Ennerdale, so I was quids in there, but I had missed the first race in Ireland so needed to make an effort with the other two.

During the week after the Ennerdale, I rested up and tried to get my back sorted out a bit. The following weekend, Mandy was away and I went for a gentle run up Skiddaw with our hound and her friend, Jake the spaniel. Trotting down the wide easy-angled path and enjoying the birds eye view over Derwentwater, I suddenly hit the ground. Ouch!! I could not get up. The dogs stood there pathetically as I lay wincing and some kind passers-by came to see what the damage was. I knew I had hurt my hand and my shoulder but could not tell how badly and which of them was worse. Lying on the ground, winded and wounded, I had only one thing on my mind and that was the Dollar Race in Scotland in seven days' time. After a few moments, I pulled myself together and reassured my Samaritans that I was alright. Slowly, I jogged back down and had to put the mutts on the lead as we went along the road, passing the cottage hospital on our way home. Luckily, the dogs did not pull. I was in two minds whether to go in the minor injuries clinic but thought better of it being covered in dirt and with two filthy dogs in tow. That afternoon my friend Annemieke turned up at my house, as we were meant to be going to a barbeque and playing volleyball. She put me in a sling, and I went to bed. It was just as well that I did not attempt the volleyball because, when I did get my x-rays on Monday, I had a dislocation of my acromioclavicular joint and a broken finger. The following Friday, I went to see Jo Gillyon. Besides being an accomplished runner, Jo is also a brilliant massage therapist. She taped up my shoulder, and the next morning we were on the road north to Dollar together with Cat. As we were warming up, I was under strict instructions: "On no account fall over. Just stay upright, and everything will be fine."

During the warm up we went to have a look at the start and finish, the latter up and down a steep muddy path through trees where there were lots of roots designed as trip hazards for those coming down at high speed. Cat observed jokingly, "Oh, I would not like to be chased downhill when it gets to this stage."

Everything was fine in terms of staying on my feet going uphill. After the half-way point, I was passed by Cat, who poked me in the arse to go faster. Towards the end my instinct was to let fly on the descent. I thought I might be better off forgetting caution and just trusting myself: after all, I stayed upright most of the time. Surely, Skiddaw had been an aberration because I was enjoying the view too much. I went for it down the hill and into the woods and noticed I was catching up on the woman in front. It was Cat, whose words came back to haunt her as I was breathing down her neck. I gave everything as I kept up the pressure but she got away at the bottom, and I could not match her on the short road run to the finish. Since Cat is a good many years younger, I was not too concerned, but I still only came in fourth in my age group. I would need a great run in Wales but arrived at the start with an awful cold and not sure if I should run. My team were there, and so was Mandy. Well, it was only a cold – I could always pull out if I was really ill, so I may as well start. Mandy headed up into the hills with various water bottles and snacks for all in the yellow and green vests of Keswick and of course Wendy Dodds: we count her as an honorary member when it comes to jelly-baby supplies. In addition to our own hound, poor Mandy also seemed to amass a large team of dogs. She carefully had them all, including Lyn Thompson's Lakeland Terrier, tethered to a rock and got herself organised to have refreshments at the ready. Mandy had been given strict instructions not to let the terrier off the lead. You can imagine her dismay when Lyn appeared at a cracking pace with said terrier attached to her bum bag.

"Mandy! How did he get loose?"

"I don't know. I think one of the other dogs must have undone his lead!"

In a comedy which reduced onlookers to fits, Lyn quickly exchanged the dog for a water bottle, and carried on running cool and calm, and still fast. In all the dog hullabaloo, Jo missed her refreshments, but we all came in safely, me in the third place in the vets to secure a British bronze medal overall; we also bagged a team bronze.

Those medals were already in the bag a couple of weeks before the race at Hodder, so, on that last sunny day, winning the vet 50 English Championship at the Hodder Show really was a lovely end to an action-packed season, and most of all it was far from Pendle. I was a long way from the negative, fearful jelly-baby I had been just five months previously. It was at that very moment, near the end of the final race at Hodder, when it all came together, that I really changed. That moment when I dared to ask if I could run even faster. To say someone gave a hundred and ten percent always seemed to me like a stupid comment before, but now I got it. I knew what it meant to feel that there was nothing left and yet to find something more. I knew what it felt like to have the confidence to back myself. This has consequences because it means that it is not always necessary to base the future on the past. This meant possibility, the possibility to live new moments unconstrained by things that had gone before. This was more than going outside my comfort zone: it was way beyond that. I ran myself out of my comfort zone and, after that, went faster to find a new comfort, a new strength, and, this time, I could not forget the lesson. Helen is right. It is not possible to predict how other people will do, and, despite all our own efforts, we can always be beaten in a race. I usually am because of the simple fact that there are people who are just better at it than I am. What I had learnt was how not to beat myself.

Twelve
Just One More Chance

I can never train as hard as I race, and, sometimes my team-mates wonder what goes on. When we train together, I try hard but cannot match most of them at interval training and hard-paced runs. Then a race day arrives, and it is almost as if a changeling appears in the stead of an old hunched woman who, at other times, struggles with getting upstairs and putting on socks. In good races, something happens, and it feels like magic. My goal has thus become to find out if there is a recipe which can help to conjure this magic, and, if I can understand the magic formula, whether I can effectively share it. Like all worthwhile endeavours, it is taking some figuring out, but I do think I am well on the way to finding my answers.

After my fantastic year in 2014 with a gold in the English and bronze in the British, what could I do but continue my quest. I planned to race both the British and English Championship races again but, ideally, concentrate on the British for the unashamed ambition of wanting to win it. As always, I had physical problems, but I was managing and, even though the first English race was a short one in Yorkshire, I stayed positive and ran with gusto, coming in as third vet 50. I was full of optimism and sensed the stars were lined up in my favour, as one day, out on a training run from our house, I fell into step with another runner going up Skiddaw. We had a chat on the trot back down, and it turned out he was from Wales, and, knowing the upcoming Welsh race in the Moelwyns well, he was able to give me useful advice about the route. The week after that, when I was on our local Barrow fell, I met a chap from Durisdeer, the venue for the Scottish race later that year. While I am not really a superstitious believer in fate, having positive expectation was a good thing. I knew that these chance encounters were simply that, but, at the same time, they encouraged me to believe that things could go my way.

Having good friends in Wales to stay with also helped, and, when it came to race day, Cathy Woodhead and her husband, David, also came out on the course to give me a drink and take pictures. The race reinforced my feeling of enjoyment in doing events that were new to me. The Welsh hills have their own atmosphere; a hint of broodiness even on a sunny day like this one. We ran up a slatey path past some old quarry workings, then along an airy ridge with some intricate ups and downs returning over grass, bog and heather. I felt I ran well, coming second in my age group. I was satisfied yet still hungered to improve. As spring burst forth, we went south to Stretton, where Jenn, Jo and I finished on top of each other. Then, there was the Duddon, which I loved and in which I came in first vet 50, the same happening in the Scottish race at Durisdeer. So, as summer approached, I was in a buoyant mood and full of excitement. I was doing well in the English races and had a first and second place out of two British races with two to go. But I was not the only one full of hopes, as Cat was now heavily pregnant and expecting the birth of her daughter at the start of July.

In calm and reflective moments, I did not *really* think I could win the British, as Liz, my main rival in this competition, was, on all the available evidence, a faster runner than me. Liz had been unable to make it to Scotland, but I knew she would still be likely to beat me in Ireland and at Lingmell in the Lake District. It was the best three races out of four that would count, but still a second place overall would be great for me. But all this was conjecture because in fact, I was heading for trouble. Around about the end of June, my back was hurting more than normal. I had had quite bad back pain for about forty years and, at school, was written off from sport because, due to a developmental disease, my thoracic spine is the wrong shape and pretty rigid. Having said that, I can normally get around the house even on a bad day, so, when that became impossible, I knew I was in trouble. As is customary in our household when I have a medical disaster, my partner, Mandy, was off in a far-flung place carrying out structural inspections of railway bridges. As I lay on the kitchen floor, the phone rang in my pocket, and I moaned something incomprehensible to Cat. Cat, who was now our Keswick Womens' captain, rang to discuss some team arrangements. Actually, I think she was trying to distract herself from the looming prospect of going into labour. Within a few minutes, Cat and her husband, Chris, were round at my house and calling a doctor. I was worried we might also need a midwife, as baby Rowan was due imminently. It was past midnight when the doctor came, but she could not really help. Still helpless on the floor, I lay on my own for a couple more hours crying until I managed to regain a modicum of emotional control. Many people will be familiar with that nasty feeling when your back *goes*. Everything spasms up, and, as the body has a mind of its own, no matter how much you try to relax, it is impossible to straighten up because moving incites a rebellion in the muscles. It is a painful, horrible and truly disabling experience. But that night on the floor was different: in comparison with previous episodes of disabling spasms, it was a different universe of pain. The recollection of it still stops me in my tracks, and I certainly have no words for it apart from, perhaps, terrifying. By the morning, I was just about able to stand and take a couple of shaky footsteps. High up on a big mountain or heading up the last hill on a long race, putting one foot in front of the other can be a huge effort, but these wobbly steps across my own kitchen floor were in a different league of difficulty from any I could remember. Despite being able to stand and becoming a little more mobile, on the whole things went from bad to worse. I became completely dependent on my friend and physical therapist Sue Read, who would come round four or five times a day to feed me and get me to the loo. My GP arranged an urgent scan, which showed a compression of my spinal cord by two large prolapsed discs. I could not feel my legs properly and was admitted to the regional neurosurgical unit as an emergency. Things were grim, but, luckily, I took a book to read. It was by the mountain-running legend Kilian Jornet, and the title was *Run or Die*.

That book was the life raft I clung to. I was fasted and put on a drip in preparation for surgery the next day. I was very scared, but I just tried to be calm and read the book. Like a helpless child, I bargained with myself and the cosmos. Please let this not happen, please can I have one more chance; I will really try, and I will not give up, if I can just have one more chance. The night passed, and I got up and wheeled my drip stand about in lieu of a morning dog walk. Hang on – it dawned on me I could walk, and almost upright! Much deliberation and discussion ensued. Neurologically, I was improving, and, due to my underlying problems, I was not a straightforward case: surgery for me would be very complex and risky. Eventually, it was decided not to rush to operate, and, after a while, I was let out on a caution to see what happened. Meanwhile, Cat had given birth to her daughter Rowan and team-mates Jo, Jenn and Rachel had organised a recce of the English race up Lingmell, so I went with them. In retrospect, I can only speculate about what I can have been thinking, but maybe I was trying not to think.

When I was in hospital, I mentioned I had some races to do, but the doctors deemed me delusional. My consultant had looked at me pityingly: "I'm not telling you not to run, it probably won't make any difference, I just don't see how you can run!". Yet back in Cumbria I had managed the recce and so I turned up for the Lingmell Race with my team. Little Jenn reminded us that it was Wimbledon finals day and that, while we laboured up the fell, Serena would be hitting aces on centre court. As we were warming up, we were mindful of what an impressive athlete Serena is and wondered if we could take some inspiration from her, so I came out with a mantra we could use.

"I'm big, I'm black, and I will *not* be beaten."

We all laughed, as none of us makes more than eight and half stone wet through, and there is unfortunately not much ethnic diversity in our team. But we embraced the spirit of Serena and set off as if we meant it. Lingmell is certainly big and steep and is one of those races ominously referred to as a *dash*, meaning straight up and down the same way, no messing. The word dash is synonymous with brutal. Coming off the summit, I saw Rowena in her orange vest and, drawing on the mantra, swept past. The team did well and came third, and I secured a silver medal in the English Championship overall. My back hurt a bit, and I had some numbness and odd jittering in my legs, but, otherwise, I was surprisingly alright.

Then for the big day – the Seven Sevens in the Mountains of Mourne, Northern Ireland. It was a simple calculation: one out of the two of us would win our race, and whoever did would win the British vet 50 championship. Since I was definitely second best even before my latest bodily misadventures, the outcome was predictable. It was a cool and breezy day, and the first climb, long and rough from sea level to Donard summit, went well. As I was coming off the second summit, the test started: Liz appeared on my shoulder. Would I give in and let her past? Simply accept the reality that I was not good enough? No, I thought – I'll just play a game. I'll pretend I am a good runner and keep ahead – all I have to do is stay in front at all times. In front is in front. I enjoyed this pretending game. Dismissing every challenge, every nip and tuck, I just put my feet back in front of hers and carried on. This continued, for several hours. Coming down Meelbeg, I was looking very closely at my feet, as, a few months earlier on the recce, I had put one down a big hole in the heather and gone in thigh-deep. Unbeknown to my companion on that recce, John Byrne, I could feel something large and furry under my leg. It's a badger, I thought, it will bite me, and I'll get TB or die of septicaemia. These thoughts were translated into screams of "Get me out, get me out!" John was worried in case I had broken my leg. Thankfully, all was well after he dragged me, and a fully-grown sheep, out of the seemingly very small hole. Looking back from Binnian, we marvelled at how many more sheep there might be hidden on that seemingly unpopulated hillside.

As I crossed the Silent Valley Dam on the actual race, I could hear Mandy and Moss the hound singing to me from further up the heathery hill. I managed to find them and took some fluids – and courage. There was a long out and back section and after the turn around point no sooner had I reset my course than Liz was again on my shoulder. It was a long way home and still one more big climb to do. I got a stone in my shoe, but getting it out would lose the race. Two, three, four steps in front. Right, I thought, all incoming sensations are now irrelevant and must just be ignored. With less than five miles to go, I swallowed one more gel, and then the only thing that mattered in the world was for me to stay ahead. I ran like a hunted animal and it was no longer a game. On the last descent, I tried a direct line to the left of the path which I had not recced but which Ed had said was faster. It was steep and rough but shorter, and I had to risk it. I popped out on the path below, three, four, five steps ahead. Tapes appeared in the woods to direct us to the finish, and Liz was right on my shoulder breathing down my neck. More effort, faster, come on I told myself as I was running along on my own red line. I reacted if it was a sprint, and as the distance opened up between us – I knew I had done it. Between gasps, I smiled. A huge track down into the park, two tapes hung on branches, stud marks down a trod in the mud between the tapes, no one ahead. Dive off here into the finish field. Oh, God! Suddenly, I was stopped, stuck in a mass of brambles. It's not this way. Run. Where? Anywhere. I scrambled out and emerged in a car boot sale. I could see the big track going straight to the finish field and ran back uphill, the searing pain in my legs just irrelevant as I saw Liz cruising in towards the finish line. As in a fall or car crash, or indeed any type of terrible accident, milliseconds turned to hours, and I knew in an instant I had given it away. I'd be too embarrassed ever to go home to Keswick. But every fibre of my unthinking being held onto another story as my legs, my lungs, my heart sprinted on to get me back on the right track one stride in front of Liz. In front again and with very little distance left, I was propelled on by some unfathomable force from within to pull away again. And it is strange how, after four hours and fifty minutes of racing, I could do a 200 metre personal best and win by twenty-one seconds.

It was Ed's fiftieth birthday. He had been given the number fifty on his vest and was celebrating with a cup of tea after his race so did not see me come in. He runs for a club called Cheshire Hill Runners and his birthday present was being part of a bronze medal winning team. Smiling with the glow of success but eager to know how I had got on, he came over. On seeing that I was not looking that happy, however, he appeared concerned, enquiring tentatively:

"Are you alright, Jules?"

"Yes, fine, wouldn't mind a cup of tea."

"I'll get you one. By the way, how did you get on?"

I was struggling to believe what I had to say, a big part of me still being held in the moment when I went wrong through the trees. Although somewhat traumatised, I nevertheless managed to get the truth out.

"I was first old woman."

"Well, there you are: a British Champion!"

Judging by the expression of pride on Ed's face, I might as well have bagged another Nobel Prize.

When I finished, Mandy was still up the mountain, but red-faced and tired, she made it back in time for prize-giving. We all say it's not about the winning, but it makes me very happy when I feel that people whom I love are proud of me. If this was all about seeking attention and approval, then perhaps it was a demonstration that I am a very insecure person, as it was some lengths to go to in order to satisfy that motive. And that would be an oversimplification. My motives were actually many, as were my rewards, and I have no shame in admitting that one reward was sharing the evening and a Guinness with Mandy and Ed and ringing up my team-mates back in Keswick. Of course, if I had come second I would be the same friend and wife and would mean no less to them, but to be able to smile and bask in each other's success is an innocent pleasure.

When I got home, my team-mates wanted to know how I had done it, and I told them it was because I had pretended I was a good runner. I had not set out with that game plan in mind, but, quite accidentally, I found it to be effective. The strategy of telling myself I was only pretending was not threatening, and, rather than challenging inner doubts, it just circumvented them. Between the last checkpoint and the end of the race, I felt spent, overheated and dehydrated, my tired muscles being on the edge of cramping, but I kept going without slowing down at all because, by that time, I was fully engaged in the race. Every fibre of my being was focused on the task of running as fast as possible. There was nothing else, no imagining the finish, no responding to pain, no thought of slowing down. Nothing existed in the world except the race, the next footstep, the next breath. Moving through time and moving through space, sensing every subtlety of the touch of my feet on the forest track, every landing and take-off, every detail of what was inside me and around me. All the things which are usually hidden in the subconscious became tangible. I knew every heartbeat, the start, the middle and the end of each inhalation, the space between the in-breath and the out-breath. I was immersed in the act of running a race, living a life.

In endurance running, there is a model of fatigue called *the central governor*, which was put forward by the famous coach and physiologist Tim Noakes. Muscles are made up of fibres, and the fibres contract when instructed by nerves. The more fibres involved the stronger the contraction. Dr Noakes and his team expected to find that, in the state of fatigue towards the end of endurance events, the nerves would recruit more of the muscle fibres to contract, drawing on any reserves in order to get the job done. They were surprised to find in their experiments that the opposite is true. As exercise progresses, the brain is less willing to send the necessary messages, and fewer and fewer muscle fibres are mobilised to undertake the task. Noakes interprets this data as evidence of a subconscious protective mechanism, the central governor, which is there to guard against pushing the heart muscle itself so hard that it goes into an oxygen deficit and endangers the life of the runner.

The hypothesis describes fatigue as an emotional response to subconscious messages from the body about how close the red line of maximum effort is. Like all responsible guardians, the governor errs on the side of caution, and its job is to produce some emotional distress well ahead of the red line in order to make the runner slow down. Noakes and others intriguingly speculate about the degree to which the governor itself can be trained to need a lesser margin of error. What seems clear to me is that the governor will not respond to bullying. The conscious mind simply does not have the authority to override it. The governor must hone its accuracy from experience. Noakes advocates this way of running using intuition honed by experience, as this is how the best seem to perform.

When fatigue rears its unwelcome head, we have choices. A common, but usually unhelpful, choice is to distract the mind with other thoughts. This can be of some use in super-long ultra-distance races, where pace needs to be pretty slow at times, but the distraction strategy is counterproductive in the last phase of most races where a reasonable speed is still desirable. If we think about a road marathon or long race on the fell such as the Wasdale, the limiting factor is not just the pace of getting to mile twenty or twenty-two, or indeed the pace of getting to Styhead Tarn: the crux is maintaining speed for the last bit. Of course, this depends not only on not tackling the first bit too fast but also on how fatigue is dealt with. Disassociating thoughts from the task may feel more tolerable and may be a way of coping, but it dilutes focus and energy. If you are thinking about what's for dinner or where you are going on your next holiday, then you are less aware of the need to correct unhelpful tension, uneconomic running style or inefficient breathing. Another option is to try self-bullying, which can produce a positive response for a very short time but is super-expensive in energy terms because it creates fear and therefore tension, and this is a waste. It is also a rather unpleasant experience. But, if neither distraction nor willpower is optimal, how do we push without pushing and get the governor to allow us to keep running fast and get even nearer to the red line of our maximum performance? Just ask. That is my suggestion based on my experience – just ask, nicely, calmly and without self-judgement. Can I run any faster? Sometimes, I find that an internalised mantra can help and play the words: *Let the runner run*. After a while, this sometimes just becomes *run*. It is not so much an urging of oneself on but a way of calming the mind without distracting its focus. If a word is too much, then there is always the breath, the next breath, and a focus on the space between the end of the out-breath and start of the in-breath. My impression is that, while the central governor can probably be trained, it cannot be effectively overridden by force of will, and trying to fight it will just store up trouble. Let the runner run. What happens if you allow yourself to run a bit faster or just invite yourself to keep going? Sometimes, what can happen is amazing, and next time you need to turn on the speed, the governor may have recalibrated itself a little.

At the Hodder Show the previous year, during the last mile of the last race of the season I had to consciously ask myself some questions:

"Do you want to win it?"

It was a yes to that: yes, I was bothered.

"Can you run any faster?"

I did not think so.

Are there any downsides to trying to run faster now, at this very moment? (Since the situation was unfolding very quickly, these thoughts were also very quick.)

I could not think of a reason not to speed up. I was very pushed, but my body knew that I still had a margin of error between me and the red line and that it was only my mind that was trying to preserve the margins. It was a question of letting my body do it, inviting myself to run faster, allowing it without trying to interfere. And breathing the best breathing possible.

In Ireland, the whole of the last part of the race was run on reflex and bodily intuition – especially after I had gone wrong at the end. My conscious mind was out of its depth and could not think fast enough to sort the situation out.

In the end, intuition and emotion are what wins races. Inborn talent is, of course, also a massive factor. While training and strategy prepare the ground and pacing is very important, we can all do those things, follow a programme, run at a certain pace, eat the right things and yet still be frustrated, knowing that there is a better run inside waiting to get out. Perhaps the reason why many of the male fell running records of the eighties and nineties have not been broken, even though many people understand the *science* of running, is that modern-day runners simply do not love it as passionately and intuitively as Billy Bland, Joss Naylor, and even Bob Graham himself. We tend to remember *the round* and forget the man, yet this plimsole clad, pyjama shirted hero was an extender of boundaries like no other.

Of course, I am not in any way an exceptional runner. I am reasonably good, but there are many exceptional people who are a lot more organised and dedicated and who simply have a great deal more genetic talent and can leave me for dust. By any realistic measure, I am respectable but mediocre. If I ever win anything, it may be down to a modicum of talent and the fact that I am not averse to the hard work needed to train, even if I do it haphazardly. But I run on the fells for one reason: I love it. It is the magic ingredient of love that has turned a misshapen old woman into a fell runner. Some people say running is pointless, but how can love be pointless? Not everyone will fall in love with the same type of person, just as we each have different things that float our particular boat. I am not sure if love can be taught, so, if a person does not love their sport, they may do well but without achieving their true best or, more importantly, having the most fun. I have met runners who are in a loveless marriage with their running, and I can see that it is hard work for them to carry on while powered by weaker motives. Even then, though, only they can judge if the rewards are enough, and I guess they still can be huge. Although it may not be possible to teach love, what can be trained is the ability to let go, engage, focus, breathe and not overthink. The best athletes have used guided imagery for decades, probably millennia actually, but how much time does the average club athlete spend on genuinely training the mind, and is every run mindful? With practice, the governor will calibrate the position of the red line of total effort more accurately. What happens when we run well is that our evolved physical intelligence is let free. It feels like magic, it feels as if a human melds with a mountain in a moment which allows both of them to express themselves.

Thirteen
A Storm in My Soul

Happiness can be a powerful anaesthetic, so, directly after the Irish race, I did not feel much pain. But I was depleted and had a nasty cold, which was a bit disappointing, as I had hoped to run in the World Masters Mountain Race in Wales. The World Masters comes to the UK only once every ten years, and, not being eager enough to travel abroad for a short race, I had never competed in it before. Now that it was coming to Wales, I felt I ought to have it on my agenda. En-route to Spain, our rock-climbing Mecca, Mandy and I went to the race in our van. I think my mind was already absorbed in the anticipation of our climbing trip. The Masters event was a mountain race in name only, turning out to be a short, well-marked trail race round a conifer wood. I was uninspired and off-colour and, ran accordingly, yet I did earn the highly amusing privilege of standing on a podium with two others, singing "God Save The Queen" for winning the team event in the over-fifty age group. Silly but fun.

After the race, we continued our journey to the unfrequented mountains of Catalunya, where there is more rock than you can shake a stick at. While we were there, I forgot about running and, on return, managed a mediocre performance in the Fell

Running Association relays, competing on a paired leg alongside Jenn Mattinson, who had to wait for me a lot but did so patiently and with much encouragement. Running had again become just too painful so I resorted back to the turbo trainer. The worst thing was that I knew, although I did not want to acknowledge it, that this pain was incomparably more intense than anything I had experienced before I was immobilised that summer. Things were very wrong, but I dared not dwell on my situation and kept insisting to myself that they would come right. After all, life was like that, wasn't it: problems would be solved simply by hard work and not giving in? A tried and tested personal strategy. Of course, I did not recommend this approach to others, but it was so engrained in my own behaviour that I could not bear to challenge it.

If I were to challenge it, I would have to give back my entry for the Tour de Helvellyn Race in December, and I had already done that twice before. Bailing out for a third time would seem like too much defeat. My approach was to just keep on with tedious training on the turbo in the garage and hope that things would come right.

In the meantime, there came another, quite different, challenge to contend with. One rainy Saturday afternoon in December 2015, I was in our garage training when, out of the corner of my eye, I noticed water coming in under the door and got off the bike to investigate. Goodness, it really was raining hard and pooling up in the back garden. Well, I couldn't do much else but put a towel across the door stoop and carry on training. Then it was time for a shower, but I hardly needed one by the time I dashed the few yards up the garden path in the deluge.

Mandy had gone down the road to visit our friends. It was dark by now, and I rang to see if they were okay. Mandy's reliable calmness and sensible instructions helped me to focus on what needed to be done.

"We are just getting everything important upstairs. Can you do the same and then come down here to help?"

I peered out the front door as the water crept ever closer, and I wondered where to start. Must save the dragon rug we carried over the pass from Ghunsa in Nepal. After gathering a few precious things and putting in place a few flimsy defences, I donned Mandy's dry suit and went off down the road – only to be met with a torrent coming over the road at the bottom of the village. The beck which would normally struggle to dampen a pair of feet was now a raging white-water river. There was no way I was going to get across that. I retreated back home and rang Mandy, who could not get back through the village so carried on helping our friends. Thankfully, the water stayed out of our house that night, although the neighbours were flooded, and the village became cut off. The next day, I set off to work, and, as I escaped from our village onto the main road, I thought I would make it. After seeing there was still a major river flowing over the debris strewn A66 at Braithwaite, I quickly reappraised the situation yet felt very guilty about my enforced absence.

Storm Desmond took its toll on our community in so many ways. We all need a safe home, but Desmond did not care about that. He just did what was in his nature to do, unleashing a deluge and devastating people's homes and belongings and sense of security. Our friendly little town looked like a disaster zone, but people worked hard, and are still working hard, so that Desmond can one day be just a bad memory.

Before dawn two weeks after the flood, I was in Askham Village Hall with my friend Sarah Bailey. The Tour de Helvellyn was going ahead. We set off across the moor on a cold windy morning, and, as Ullswater came into view, it looked more like the Atlantic, with white horses leaping on a heaving grey swell. As we battled on against the gale, progress was further slowed by our having to wade over great landslides of deep alluvial mud, which had been washed down by Desmond. Sinking into the glutinous stuff felt horrible, but the effort of pulling each leg out to take another hard-won step was worse. I was desperate to avoid the unthinkable disaster of falling head first into the gloop and imagined a series of statues of runners rendered solid inside a thick encasement of hardened clay along the path to Howtown. We could be immortalised like an Anthony Gormley installation, and people would come from all over the world to see us in decades to come. Once we reached Howtown, things were relatively civilised, and the run up Boredale and over Boredale Hause to Patterdale was much easier, with a nice cup of tea and some food being a lovely encouragement at Side Farm. By contrast, the run up to Sticks Pass was laborious, but there was a jolly atmosphere and lots of chat with fellow runners. Going through the woods on the west side of Helvellyn, I could see that Desmond had laid more traps – this time in the form of washed-out streams, which were still raging torrents. Luckily, Mandy had gone along there to cheer me on, and assisted by several competitors, had attended to the most ferocious river, securing a huge log in place to aid crossing. Having met her and Moss on the track, I heeded the warning to be careful because they had only just made it back across the water. Faced with the fearful torrent, I waited for the people behind me. I was glad I had not dared to risk the crossing alone, as, without their help, I might have been swept away to a nasty end. But best not to dwell on near-misses, so I pushed on but at the next river I could not face another scary crossing: my two helpers had run on ahead, and I decided to take a detour round to the road and up to Dunmail Raise. Worn down and depleted by the gale after more than four hours out, I consoled myself with the thought that, after the next hill up to Grisedale Tarn, the wind would at last be on my back. At the top, I picked up the boggy grass trod around the tarn edge, getting a shower from the windblown spray into the bargain. It can be a test of character when something looked forward to longingly turns out to be a bitter disappointment. The following wind proved to be not a kindly helper but a malevolent beast, whisking me off my feet on the rocky descent. Time without number, I threw myself to the ground rather than risk being bashed against rocks or blown, out of control, over a craggy edge. My hat being plucked from my head was an annoyance rather than a tragedy, as it was a one-euro special from Decathlon. Perhaps a Herdwick could make use of it. With me safely in the valley at last, it was now just a case of getting some more food and drink down and plodding on. Another detour due to Desmond damage added more miles, and the race turned from the billed thirty-eight to more like my favoured forty-two. Joining the outward route again at Side Farm, the tea was now more of a lifesaving elixir than a mere comfort, and there was still a long way to go, retracing our morning steps back to Askham. At Howtown, Mandy met me with more hot drink before, in gathering gloom, it was time to renegotiate the mud slides. I had learnt the route over the moor, so the impending dark was not a worry, and I was still managing to keep up a trot while mentally ticking off the memorised landmarks and trod junctions. Trotting was the only option, as my legs were in a right state, especially the left one, and, if I had stopped to walk, it felt as if I may as well stop to die. Trying to relax can be a good pain management strategy, and the only thing I could think of was to sing, loudly. A version of Simon and Garfunkel's *Homeward Bound* came belting out, and I kept up the tuneless chant all the way to the road into the village until I realised that I had been followed. A bloke, who was obviously in a much better state than me but not as confident with the route, ran past and thanked me for showing him the way. Over the moor, I had, in fact, had a feeling I was being shadowed but, in near darkness, did not look, as I thought it was just the eerie atmosphere. He must have thought I was nuts. I felt embarrassed as my singing is not up to much at the best of times. It being only a day or two from the winter solstice, blackness won its claim on the world as my feet found the tarmac into the village. At the end of the street, I hesitated: I was sure there had been a village hall here this morning. Then I noticed a thin door-shaped rim of light and, after tentatively trying the handle, fell into a different world altogether: that of hubbub, tired runners and hot cups of tea. I had only just made it in without needing to fumble with a headtorch. A very cold Sarah came in a while later after having run with her friend Ian Grimshaw, who had lost his torch. They had been on the moor in the dark and had to navigate with just one light. It was an ace-of-spades night out there. I am not sure how they had managed.

So that was the end of 2015, and the year which followed was grim for me. Not a single race and very few runs. What had I been thinking of to set out on the Tour de Helvellyn in pain before I even started and knowing it would only get worse? I am ashamed of myself now because, although I did enjoy the day, the adventure and the sense of achievement, I knowingly went out and harmed myself. What made me do this? I had worried that life would be dull without racing, that I would be somehow lost or lose a part of me if I could not run. It was clear that I needed to stop, as I was already lost. It's no longer life-enhancing to carry on when the body just cannot do it and simply needs to heal. Then, although I did not run at all, things went from bad to worse, and I stopped being able to even walk on the fells. I could not sleep, as lying down hurt. Sitting down at work hurt. Driving hurt. Walking hurt, and, after a while, just living hurt. Survival became a daily challenge. I knew I could not sustain this: things needed to change. I would either go mad or become completely disabled – or both. From head to foot, I was full of tension and pain. I was now my own patient and I was the only person who could really change my fate.

Complex problems rarely succumb to simple solutions. As medical practitioners, we are urged to subscribe to the Occam's razor principle, also known as 'the law of parsimony', which essentially states that, in the face of different explanations, the simplest one should be preferred. Yet, in my experience, we can easily be made into simpletons by buying into over-simplistic explanations. There are indeed plenty of reasons why my shoulder, neck, back, hips and legs should hurt. For a start, my spine failed to develop normally. Maybe the large prolapsed discs pressing on my spinal cord and nerve roots add to my trouble, but to what extent cannot be really known. Over the years, I had become quite skilled in pain management, but, since the episode on the kitchen floor, nothing had ever been the same. Except for that brief window when I won my age group in the Irish race, my legs hadn't even felt as if they belonged to me the way they had before. I struggle to explain what happened to allow me to run like that in Ireland. It is hard to believe that I could numb myself so much simply because I wanted to race. I suppose it is just another piece of evidence that the experience of pain is entirely dependent on context. The truth is that I was in a hell of a mess, and, since it had taken decades of overlapping issues to get me there, I sensed that there would not be a simple solution. The thing I have never bought into is that there is no solution. I was offered surgery on my back again and, again, after more deliberation, put it on the back burner, deciding that it would be a last resort and that I had a lot more resorts yet to explore. Pain can be a useful signal, but it can also be a *cry wolf*. When pain has become learnt by the spinal cord and brain and when all those pain fibres have been exercised and strengthened over months and years, it is truly impossible to know what the message of the pain is any more. Often, it can become like a faulty warning light coming on at the slightest provocation when there is nothing really wrong, but how can we know what the meaning is when all you get to know is the pain?

In our village, we are lucky enough to have a great village hall, where Tray, our wonderful yoga teacher, comes every week to help us to open our chakras, floss our joints and rebalance our bodies and minds. Tray has a lot of running disciples locally, and I am among them. I had not been going to classes long when, one evening during the relaxation at the end of the session, I had a strange experience of feeling as if my body was lying still on the floor relaxing while I was looking down from the ceiling. This was very pleasant but afterwards slightly disturbing to one who struggles with any concept that we have a spirit or energy separate from our physical body. The motto on the Long-Distance Walkers' Association's website, which states that "the body is largely a vehicle for the will", does not coincide with my own take on things. I concede that it feels as if we have a separate will, but I do not believe we *really* do. There are no separate parts to me: I am one animal.

Being related to dreaming, out-of-body experiences are, in fact, not that uncommon and can be induced by various drugs, sleep deprivation and both extreme stress and extreme relaxation. Working alternate day and night shifts had not been healthy in the long run, and, when I started that yoga class, I was tired and stressed, but, by the end, I was deeply relaxed. I was amazed at my reaction to the relaxation and became gradually aware of just how tense my baseline mode of living had become. Interestingly, it was my body that had this insight – not my analytic mind. Bodies often pay the price for overworked and unbalanced minds. The work of the psychiatrist Bessel Van de Kolk documenting the long-term physical effects of psychological trauma is both fascinating and sobering. Fear, angst, trepidation and wariness are all learnt in our bodies, and it is in our bodies that we need to learn to feel safe, relaxed and at ease. Maybe my body was so worn out that there was no sense of ease to be had, so the ceiling was the only place where I could relax.

Yoga sparked off within me a sense of hope that I could reconcile my inner conflicts and that, somehow, my ailing body would respond and heal if given help. Ever since I fell over on Skiddaw and dislocated my acromioclavicular joint, I was in denial about my left shoulder. I had never been able to extend that joint very well due to my wonky anatomy, and falling over at the Calderdale Relay had not helped either. It was too stiff and painful for me to even attempt exercising it, so, again, I followed my ignore-and-carry-on policy. It was too inconvenient and required too much energy to do anything else.

Like a stubbornly reluctant beast gently led by the nose, I went along with yoga, and gradually it began to affect me. Over weeks and months, my sense of what neurologists refer to as interoception was awakened. Interoception is the ability to sense what is going on inside one's own body. In common with other children who had grown up in a terrifying environment, powerless to influence or escape, I became shut off from my inner feelings. Shutting off the sick and panicky physical feelings of fear inside is in itself a survival mechanism. It is also a problem, and one that can lead down a variety of self-destructive paths. There are many different ways of trying to block out one's feelings. Yet I had been lucky to discover climbing and running and these activities had, to some extent, restored a healthy balance to my body, at times putting me back in tune with myself, but only up to a point. When something was amiss, especially in running, I found it easier to carry on than pay too much attention. I am not the first runner to find it hard to come to terms with injuries and physical shortcomings, which prevent the external expression of our joyous, deeply-ingrained impulse to run. Only now can I begin to see that coming to terms with my own weaknesses is a really useful process. In yoga, I began to notice which bits of me were tense and sore and which tight bits seemed to create pain elsewhere. I began to get what people meant when they would say "listen to your body".

Differentiating between useful and useless pain is an important skill. Contemporary understanding of pain is still largely based on the work of Melzack and Wall, particularly on their 1982 classic book *The Challenge of Pain*. Having recently reread it, I found eloquent descriptions of concepts around the usefulness, or otherwise, of pain. Although pain definitely has a protective function, when a person is, as I seemed to have been, riddled with pain every day for months, running into years, it seems to turn into a useless and diminishing pain. Melzack and Wall describe such chronic pain as "a normally adaptive mechanism which has run amok". When it comes to pain, bodies seem to like to remember it, and the nerves that carry pain signals can be strengthened with use, so that, even long after an injury has actually healed, pain can still be felt. Learning how to interpret the meaning of pain and how to respond constructively to it is tricky. Personally, I have found that the first useful step is to quit fighting. I would usually respond to pain by running away from, and ignoring, it or entering into an aggressive battle against it, showing it who the boss is around here. Although it would be an exaggeration to say that I have made friends with my pain, I have at least gone to arbitration. I have learnt to be my own arbiter by trying to stay calm and asking the pain what it wants. While this is not always the case, at times just asking it, without too much prejudgement or emotion, seems to get it to quieten considerably. Maybe it wants me to move or stretch or relax and rest. Maybe it wants me to reorganise my priorities to suit my own values and meanings in life instead of trying to live on terms dictated to me. Or perhaps the pain is asking me to let go of the story of my inner *badness* and inadequacy. Understanding that I was missing my interoceptive sense I have begun to interpret my internal workings in ways which are bearing fruit – slowly. This wonky body is asking for trust that, if I do what it calls for and create a sense of relaxation and safety inside myself, then I will feel better.

My back problem, called Scheuermann's Disease or Juvenile Osteochondrosis, is common but under-diagnosed, and there is little effective help available on the NHS. This is sad, as a lot of suffering could be avoided if specialist physiotherapy were available to teenagers with the condition. To this day, the disease is often dismissed as trivial by some medics in the UK who do not understand the impact it can, and does, have – a situation I find frustrating. The severity of the disease varies, but I can say that ever since primary school I have not been able to move like my friends. I have always been a weird shape and I have always had back pain. Recently, a doctor friend of mine suffering from a similar condition tracked down one of the few physiotherapists in the UK who are trained in the Schroth Method, which is widely available in Germany. The postural exercises this practitioner taught us were really useful, although they would have been more effective if we had learnt them decades earlier. Similarly beneficial has been the work of my great friend and Alexander Technique teacher, Wyn Clayton. I have also had some hypnotherapy but found that this did not add much to the things that Tray had taught me in yoga classes and to what I had learnt about relaxation through my own training as a Human Givens practitioner. Armed with all this new knowledge and insight, I feel it's down to me now to put it into practice and work with what I have got instead of struggling against myself. It is good to know that I have not yet made the most of these practices and that, if I devote more time to them, there may be more rewards to come. The hardest part of this is not the summoning of the self-discipline to do hours of physical therapy each day, not the loss of racing, not the feeling weak, the inability to do things or even the sleepless nights and gnawing pain. The hardest part is trying not to be afraid. Asking myself what it is that I am afraid of is in itself deeply unsettling, and the answer even more so, as it turns out that the answer is myself. I am afraid in case I cannot live up to my own expectations and, most of all, that, if I lose some of the things that are closest to my heart, fell running and climbing, I may lose my heart itself. I am reminded by the writings of the great yogic traditions that difficulties are really opportunities, invitations into the unknown, but I am frightened of losing my attachments and of feeling cast adrift. I am frightened of once again feeling homeless, without a place in the world I recognise and feel safe in. I want to hang onto what is precious to me. I am a fell runner and a climber, and I live in Keswick under Skiddaw with my wife Mandy and Moss the hound, and I like it.

It is said that self-awareness is the key to healing, and I think this holds true for healing the body as well as the mind. Of course, I consider it a folly to make a distinction between body and mind, but the very way language is structured pushes us into thinking like that. The English language encourages us to divide ourselves into emotions, thoughts, body parts, mind, will and even something called soul or spirit. These distinctions are illusory, since each of us is a unique and whole person. Nothing more and nothing less – bits of us do not have a life of their own. To make an adversary of my own body would be to appoint myself my own worst enemy. My yoga mat, which is a pale purple colour, is the forum where the competing parts of myself can meet in calmness and agree to work together. I can stay with myself and not be scared off up to the ceiling. I no longer feel disappointed in my body, for to continue in that vein would be to condemn myself to never finding ease. Ease will come only when I am whole, and being bent is no reason to be divided and conflicted within myself. What I have learnt is that the more tension, worry and fear are present, the more things hurt. What it comes down to is that our bodies give us signals which we can interpret as pain, and the severity of this pain is always increased by feeling threatened. That is the point of pain: to help us assess threats to our safety and wellbeing. There is no such thing as real or imagined pain: all pain is made in our brains as a response to how much threat is being perceived. My job, then, is to create a feeling of safety within myself. Willpower and tenacity are the wrong tools for this job which requires compassion. I glance up at Skiddaw for help. She's still there.

While I am not a religious person, there are verses in the Bible that resonate with me, and I particularly love the stained-glass window in St Olaf's Church, Wasdale, with the inscription "I will lift up mine eyes unto the hills from whence cometh my strength". To the very troubled teenager and young adult that I was, the hills were the only place I ever felt strong, and I think that, without the mountains, I may never have known I had any strength. I used to think that it was their strength, the mountains' energy, that I was stealing or being given. Now the way I experience it is like a resonance: the mountains emit a strong vibe and cause me to fall into synchrony, tuning to their powerful wavelength and working on the same frequency. From the island of my yoga mat, physically troubled but gradually improving, I am minded to remember a poem which came to me on my first Alpine climbing holiday decades ago.

A View From The Bertol Hut

I see this clearly now
up here where things are simple,
blue sky, making no apology for its blueness
no veils and clouds to hide behind
no excuses.

These strong rock characters
which stand around us now,
don't bend down to avoid the wind.
An unrelenting gnawing eats into their substance,
Ice, sunshine, water...
The rock falls, the icefalls
like leaves from a tree or the shedding of tears,
these are the events of life we cannot complain at.

These strong rock characters
which stand around us now.
If we can have anything to say to each other
it would be a communication
of the necessity to accept our situation.
We must find within each of us
what is beautiful.
Beaten, broken
struck by lightning,
but not bending down
to avoid the wind.

I find it a little odd that I could write something decades ago and only now find a new meaning in it. The possibility that self-acceptance does not have to come hand in hand with frustration at my own weakness. For most of 2016, I could not run, and, for several months, I could not even do half a day's walk on the fells without being in tears with pain. Some friends wondered how I would cope, and I must admit that, on occasion, there were tears of disappointment and frustration as well as of pain. I was in a no-woman's land of not knowing what to expect. Neuropathic pain is not an area which conventional medicine generally does well in, and so, like thousands of other sufferers with these types of problems, I began to write my own manual. It was not just that I did not know whether to expect the terrible physical prognosis that experts had given me to come to pass: I also could not know how I would feel, how I would cope. I have been defensive against the idea that I was addicted to running, although, in the narrow binary terms in which addiction is most often framed, it is an accurate assertion. Life is never that simple, and addiction is not actually a simple black-and-white issue. Wherever there is pleasure, there is potential for addiction, which is one of the reasons why marketing works and why healthy things such as sex, food, a good glass of wine or a nice cup of tea can become addictive. Addiction is not all or nothing: it is possible to have a weak addiction or a strong addiction, and, because my love of running was strong, did this indicate a big problem? Breaking addiction is considered a good thing because it puts a person back in control of themselves. Through running, I had learnt a lot about emotional and physical control, but had the very source of my help now become my downfall? I did not know what giving up running would feel like, nor did I know how all the other major changes I had to make would feel. It is not uncommon for people who have come through a medical disaster that has caused a root-and-branch revaluation and reorganisation of life to say things like "That heart attack was the best thing that ever happened to me". If signals are headed and acted upon wisely then life can improve immensely. I cannot say that my back problems are life enhancing and I would rather have lived without them. In the end though, they have led me down a path where there is more self-acceptance and compassion than I might have otherwise experienced. I stopped running because I had to: I simply had no choice in the matter. Eventually, I came to my senses and decided to take a proper break from work, having been off for less than three weeks in the first instance after the night on the floor and the subsequent trip to hospital. It was clear that, if I were to have any hope of getting out of the torture pit of physical pain, I needed to change my life. Slowly, I began to accept my situation and learn a different approach. I found that I could live without running and still be emotionally settled, and I did not experience either physical or psychological withdrawal symptoms. I have become focused on a more pressing need: to develop the skills to look after myself properly. When it comes to having a happy life, missing running is not trivial, but neither is it a deal breaker. And so, I am cultivating a new, much more compassionate, inner relationship with myself. I still have so many rich sources of joy, and there are different ways in which I can express my creativity. The ways of healing myself which I have found do take time and patience. I am, however, developing the self-control to know when I am crossing my red lines, and this is very useful knowledge. The red lines of danger are real. I argue that we often steer so far away from our limits that we can weaken ourselves and turn life insipid. Yet even I have to acknowledge one can make the opposite mistake. Sometimes it pays to stop and reflect. In doing so I have found an immense, almost overwhelming, sense of gratitude for my life.

2016 came to an end, and, in the last hour of that year, I put on a wetsuit and, together with Mandy and her niece Sian, waddled along the road to a New Year Eve's party at the marina. Our friends counted out the year as we three ran along the shore in the rain and plunged into the lake for a swim. Fireworks exploded colour into the inky sky above us as midnight struck, and we tried to catch our breath as the icy water shocked our bodies. A new year began, and we ran into the warm for bubbly. Already, I had a new ambition.

"I would love to swim front crawl to St Herbert's Island this year."

"Oh great," replied Sue, our host and a very proficient swimmer. "We'll start training when it's a bit warmer!"

Fourteen

Life, the Universe and Fell Running

Spring 2017 – it was the sort of day you want to put in a bottle and keep. I had been away from home for a week of studying and early in the morning I was driving back up the motorway. As the fells came into view, I was surprised and excited to see them gleaming with a fresh covering of brilliant snow. I was eager to get home and get out. It was the last Saturday in March, the day of the Causey Pike Race in the Newlands Valley, a couple of miles from our house. Mandy was going to walk up to marshal on the summit with our dog, Moss. At first I was intending to join them, but a different urge was stirring within me and I couldn't ignore it.

"Mandy, should I come with you or run?"

"It's up to you, dear. We'll be fine if you want to run, but will you?"

I had no answer. Would I be fine? Over the previous few weeks, I had done only a few tentative, short runs, nothing requiring effort except for a couple of park runs on the flat, and no race for nearly eighteen months. Would I? The Causey Race is only four and half miles, but it packs a punch. Who cares if I come last, anyway? I just wanted to see what it would feel like, and I would stop if I needed to. Besides, I could always walk. After everything that had happened, I did not dare to hope that I might race again. For so long, this had been downright impossible.

We arrived early so that Mandy could set off to the top to get into position for her marshalling duty. I did some yoga in the parking field and relaxed in the warm spring sun next to the comforting burble of the crystal-clear beck. It's good to get some vitamin D at this time of year. Birds were singing and daffodils were dancing along the verges and lambs (yes, I have to admit they are cute!) were gambolling on fresh green carpets of spring grass. The blue sky was bright and bold with sunshine reflected from the white blanket of snow spread over all the fell tops. I was breathing in draughts of paradise. After stretching and relaxing I sauntered over to the race registration where I bumped into my old friend Lindsay Buck, who is an inspiration because she adores the fells and keeps on running year in, year out, having done so for decades, relentlessly, just because she loves it. We sat on a bench outside the village hall, absorbing the glory of the day, and I felt reassured.

Warm up then, I thought to myself, and, after a gentle jog up and down the road, I settled to the start. On this race, there is about fifty metres of flat running and then its straight up: steep then steeper. I was surprised that it seemed easy to steady my breathing and make good progress. A few minutes in, and people tend to settle into place according to pace, and I found myself running with my team-mate Rachel Mellor, whose friendly "Go on, Jules" helped me to maintain a really good rhythm. Rachel overtook me before the summit, and I popped up to greet Mandy, our exchange of "Hello, dear" being as serene and happy as the day itself. At the top of the steep bit of the descent, I had a moment of panic. The slithery grass was covered in wet snow. Oh, bugger, how do you do this downhill running thing again? I tried to relax and focus on my foot landings and, thankfully, emerged safely on the track back to Stair. My left shoulder hurt, but I breathed the tension away and made sure I picked up my feet on the awkward bouldery path. At the beck crossing, I plunged thigh-deep into the cold, clear water, but there was no time to linger. On this astonishingly beautiful day, it was astonishing that I was racing. At the finish, I had a quiet tear and a big smile. Despite running as best I could, I was a whole lot slower than in former times – yet I felt brilliant. Indescribably brilliant. If judged by time, it is possibly my worst ever race, but, on every other measure, it ranks with the very best.

I had graduated from a child in a sweetshop to being a connoisseur of special pleasures. The chance to run at Causey was extremely precious, and, although I could not lie down comfortably for the next couple of nights, I recovered after a few days. If I play my cards right, there might be a chance of doing the odd race, but this will need to be handled carefully. Rare things such as this need to be savoured like good food and fine wine, their every moment, footstep and breath being delicious. My days of gluttony are over.

No matter what the future holds, no matter if there ever is another run or race, I realise that, as well as having had a brilliant time while fell running, I have learnt a few things too. Learning is acquiring an amalgam of passed-on knowledge and personal experience. Sound training plans, good nutrition and attention to rest and general body maintenance are all tried and tested to make a difference to performance. But in attempting to get to grips with the basics of sport psychology, I have found some of the prevailing dictums to be far removed from my real experience. Almost every text you ever read about performance in sport makes a big deal out of what is termed *the arousal curve*. The idea is that, if you are either too aroused or not aroused enough, then performance will suffer, the sweet spot being somewhere in the middle. Too laid back or too worked up; neither is a recipe for success. It is not that this thesis is entirely wrong but it just isn't all that helpful to many people, as there is often confusion about what exactly is meant by arousal, which is usually confused with *nerves*. Arousal is a state of physiology where you are switched on and ready. It involves hormones such as adrenalin and cortisol and results in increasing the heart rate, in redirecting the flow of blood to muscles and in various changes to energy metabolism. It can also make you feel *nervous* – but only if you choose to interpret the stimuli in that way. Arousal is a physiological state and feeling nervous is only one potential emotional interpretation of that state. The failure to make that important distinction is what leads some athletes to conclude that they *need* some nerves but not to be *too nervous*. This confused interpretation is echoed by the assertion made by some coaches in both climbing and running that "fear is too much excitement". To me, this analysis is profoundly perplexing. I am very familiar with both emotions, which are as opposite as any two things can be. Fear is a fundamental animal emotion essential to keep us safe in the face of threats by causing an immediate impulse to run away fast, to turn and fight or to freeze. Excitement is experiencing an emotion of deep desire. The difference between excitement and fear is the difference between wanting to run headlong towards something and fully embrace it or wanting to run away at high speed. You can wet yourself with both fear and excitement: there are physiological overlaps in the mechanism, but the impulses, the motives, are opposite. Fear is a nasty sharp stick – excitement a delicious sweet carrot. You can run fast in fear, which may keep you safe in a moment of danger, but the stress hormones produced are not that healthy in the long term. There are all sorts of consequences for health if fear is a frequent experience, and it is also a profoundly unpleasant emotion. Although excitement can involve adrenalin, it also involves the anticipation of a reward, and to seek rewards in life is not just healthy – it is essential. It is much healthier to be a supreme, wily hunter than to be the prey that is running scared. I have never found it a very helpful suggestion that, to perform well, we need to be like Goldilocks and have a little fear but not too much. One thing that makes races such fun is that no amount of excitement is too much, and, since excitement is the opposite of fear, the latter does not need to get a look in.

What I would like to suggest is that fear is unnecessary in sport. After all, sport is a game – not a battlefield or a jungle full of savage animals, however much some sports may resemble those. A person who gets up at dawn to train, sacrifices their social life, sticks to a stringent diet, experiences bodily pain and exhaustion on a daily basis in order to excel as an athlete may not thank anyone for pointing out that "It's only a race". On the other hand, they may appreciate being told that they do not have to feel a load of unpleasant nerves and fear in order to perform at their very best. In fact, it would help them not to.

For me, the crucial insight which allowed me to feel the full joy of competing was when the penny dropped: that the butterflies in the stomach, the tingling of the skin, the inability for my thinking brain to do anything more demanding than directing me to tie my own shoelaces is not fear. It is my body getting ready to do something wonderful. It is my body getting ready to run because it wants to, because I want to, because I love running. It is not my body getting ready to run away from failure, competitors or showing myself up – and it most certainly is not some way of acting out a deep-seated need to run away from past traumas. I find such psychologising ludicrous and insulting. The thing about running is that I like it. I mean I really like it. My body knows what it needs to do to get ready for a good run because I am a runner: it's in my bones. When my veins are coursing with adrenalin it is possible to enjoy those physical feelings that once might have been interpreted as nerves, or even fear, and to relax in the deepest reaches of my mind, trusting entirely that the runner will run. This is not a Goldilocks solution of having not too much and not too little fear: it's so much better than that. It's the having-your-cake-and-eating-it solution. Once it is possible to relax into the physical feelings of arousal, then they hold no fear. It is thus possible to have as much arousal as needed and still feel unthreatened at the same time. You can even vomit because of adrenalin and feel calm about it, although it's not great for hydration. And another thing: when it comes to physical readiness, it's best to get the timing right, so that you don't pull the bedroom windows off their hinges on the morning of a race.

It is said that performance in British cycling was transformed by the input of the psychologist Steve Peters, author of *The Chimp Paradox*. One of the key insights explained in his book is that the thoughtful logical human can be hijacked by their own emotions – the chimp – and that we all need to develop a *chimp management system*. The emotionally driven side of human nature, characterised by the chimp, is portrayed as childish and unsophisticated in comparison with the more grown-up think-ing and analysing parts of our nature, which Peters refers to as the human and the computer. Peters describes very neatly the type of methods which can be used both to put the thinking mind in charge of the chimp and to utilise computer functions of our brain. The aim is to put our calm and thoughtful human in the driving seat, so that our powerful but potentially unruly emotions do not derail us from whatever task we are trying to apply ourselves to. Peters draws attention to the fact that chimps are stronger than humans. The idea that our emotions have much more power than our thoughts is not new and was well described by Daniel Goleman in his classic work *Emotional Intelligence*. The work of both Goleman and Peters is excellent and very useful. What is now apparent from the findings of modern brain science is that emotions always come first in the sense that it simply takes the brain a lot longer to consciously think than it does for an emotion to occur. The chimp is not only stronger it is also quicker to act. Although we are talking about the difference between milliseconds and seconds, it is nonetheless an important margin. The fact that feelings get a head start means that they often steer, or even underpin, what is consciously thought. A good example of this is that prisoners are more likely to be allowed bail when the judge has eaten than just before mealtime. Judges are more comfortable when not hungry which leads them to feel that the individual in front of them is less threatening. Realising that we are not nearly as logical as we often give ourselves credit for adds weight to Peters's assertion that, without careful effort, emotions can rule the roost with entirely unintended consequences. Certainly, we need a very good emotional intelligence to avoid being at the mercy of overwhelming feelings and deluding ourselves that our choices are considered and logical when they are really a product of the emotional stew which they were cooked in. Emotional intelligence is something which can be learnt, although on the whole, it's not a book-reading kind of learning that is required. It is not the subjugation of emotion to logic but an awareness and knowledge about our feelings and can only be acquired through experience and reflection. Through awareness we can learn to influence our own emotions but we can never write our feelings out of our script. Humans are simply not made that way.

It may be considered splitting hairs, but, as much as I think that the chimp model is very useful, one of the bits that slightly bothers me is the *I* part. Come on now, the philosophical nature of selfhood cannot have anything to do with fell running – surely. Well, the reason it does is that it is not the *human* (the real, thinking person) or the analytic *computer* that wins the race: it's the power monkey. Admittedly, it has help from the other departments, but, on those last breathless, wobbly-legged, gasping moments of a race, only the monkey has the ability to access the energy needed to get across the line. I don't know about you, but I would feel a bit cheated if all my achievements were down to some naughty chimp. *I* did that. The me of me is just as much the chimp as the computer and the human, and I won't have some little monkey stealing *my* glory.

Peters does talk about getting the chimp to work with the human, in other words not letting emotionally driven, and to some extent unconscious, agendas which we have not actively chosen, to take over control. These are sound ideas, but I would like to put a special word in for *the chimp* here and suggest that the chimp does not deserve her implied status lower down the hierarchy than the controlling human. And chimp nurturing is subtly but importantly different from *management*. This nuance is analogous to a marriage. I would rather feel nurtured by my wife than managed by her! The importance of the difference lies in the fact that emotions are the source of our motivation in the first place; the words even have the same linguistic root. Without motivation provided by emotion, there is no reason to bother: the chimp is our life force. In the end, I have to reject Peters's slightly negative imagery of our emotional selves as being cast as a naughty chimp. The fact that I hold such a deep respect for my emotional self and recognise that it is the source of all my energy and creativity is why I am, physically and otherwise, capable of so much more than my logical mind would ever allow. Imagination is not only more powerful than willpower, it is also richer. It is the creative flow of imagination, powered by the inner story-teller, that opens up possibilities in our lives. Like a wellspring which bubbles up on the fell, from a coalescence of under-ground veins, our imagination emerges from a coalescence of emotions, memories and ideas to enable us to pen the next sentence, chapter and sometimes even a verse. Cool analytical thinking, iron forged willpower, cannot write poetry or the next meaningful page of a human story. Imagination, which draws on all parts of us, is where we create our problems and sometimes where, most beautifully and masterfully, we solve them.

When Noakes talks about training our intuition through experience he is talking about acquiring a kind of whole-self wisdom that is not a matter of putting logic in control. It cannot be done through dividing ourselves into a hierarchy of depart-ments. We can delude ourselves that human life does not need to involve some pain and suffering and we can delude ourselves that we can act on reason untainted by feeling. These choices are not mine because for me they do not equate to wisdom.

Along with many other experts, Billy Bland has pointed out that, if we exclude the tiny handful of top endurance athletes, then performance in long-distance running both on and off road has been in decline for twenty years or more. Could it be that we have subtly been so influenced by a *culture of management* that we are stifling our own creativity by managing instead of nurturing our feelings and motives? Even the famous marathon coach Jack Daniels has speculated on this, calling it a "lack of guts" in modern runners. All managers who are successful in human terms know that being authoritarian and dogmatic is counterproductive. To run a good race is as much an artistic expression as any creative endeavour, such as painting, poetry or music. We may be ahead on the science of running, but are we losing the art? (I could say the same about medicine, but that is another story!)

Discussing motivation and meaning leads us to question the very nature of what we are. It is a matter of much speculation and philosophical debate as to whether the quest for a mechanism to explain consciousness will ever be fully realised. The concept of an *observing self* was an attempt to explain what consciousness is – except that it doesn't. This does not make it a useless idea, although the neurologist Bruce Hood does point out that our sense of self is somewhat of an illusion, i.e. not quite what it seems. We can experience our sense of self in different ways and one way that can sometimes be useful is when we become the observer. This was described to me by Sam, who said that, when she was flowing in a race, it was almost like watching herself perform in a film. This is very similar to other descriptions of being in the flow given by artists and performers across all disciplines. The whole of their energy is focused, but there still seems to be an observer who is simply there to enjoy the ride. I would speculate that this may be because, although the thinking, decision-making functions of the brain are not that much involved in flow experiences, awareness is not shut down altogether. The conscious brain thus almost becomes an astonished spectator, rather like a parent when their offspring suddenly does something incredibly grown up and impressive. The observing self is not a part of us, it is more a state of experiencing which we can get into at certain times. It is testament to the fact that there is a lot more to being human than being intellectually clever. We need also to be clever enough to know when simply to allow and to trust ourselves to perform. Let the runner run.

The most fundamental key to allowing total focus and complete calm to co-exist is breathing. Mandy once told me that, in climbing, there is always something you can do with your feet to make things better, and I feel that, in running as well as in climbing, there is always something you can do with your breathing things better too. Breathing is always a very good place to start when nervous interpretations of bodily arousal start to arrive. In terms of physiology the out-breath provides feedback to our nervous system to calm the flight or fight reaction and turn down adrenalin production. Breathing is fundamental and automatic, yet it can also be kept under conscious control. Making the out-breath longer than the in-breath turns adrenalin down which can be useful in all sorts of situations not just in sport. Accomplished meditators can gain control over their heart rate, blood pressure, temperature and other basic functions, but, for most of us, breathing is the most accessible way in which our conscious mind can connect with our basic bodily functions. Even in the heat of a race, if things get out of hand, then just very slightly slowing down the out-breath can bring back smooth, efficient, flowing running. Mastery of these skills needs constant practice. Handily no matter what we are doing we need to breathe so there is plenty of opportunity for such practice.

We are now back at the beginning, back to flow. Flow is about releasing the floodgates of positive power and the willingness to trust one's own creative energy enough to let the whole self be swept along. Trust is a big word, and I use it like an internally whispered mantra at times: *Trust yourself, Jules.*

Sensible, logical people would not go running up and down mountains and push each other to their physical and mental limits in all types of weather to be rewarded, at best, with an unhealthy snack and a tepid cup of tea or to win a pitifully small voucher for a local sports shop. Sensible, logical people would just not know how to have that much fun. By the way, some of the folks who win the vouchers are world-class athletes. Looking back at the years since Kit died, and at when I was doing the Bob Graham Round, I feel both sad and happy, but, above all, I feel ridiculously lucky. Not simply lucky in circumstances, in love and friendships, although no one could have been more fortunate in these, but also in finding within myself some good stuff and in being able to express it, seeing it coming alive. To quote Csikszentmihalyi directly: "The best strategy for enjoying life is to develop whatever skills one has and to use them as fully as possible." *Fully*, mind you – not just a bit.

It may be that people always think that the times they themselves live in are special, but it does seem to me that we live in a very interesting phase of evolution. We live in the age of the algorithm, where it is the expressed aim of the powerful and rich transhumanist movement to reduce all decision-making to a much more efficient version than any we can muster without technology and indeed to make death itself a thing of the past. This zeitgeist is subject to the illusion that machines can do better than humans in every field and that we ourselves are only actually a data set which could be uploaded to a different, more reliable, medium than our vulnerable bodies. It may sound like fiction, but some people are devoting their lives, and billions of dollars, to the pursuit of this vision. At the risk of sounding like a Luddite, I have to say that they have missed the point. I rather side with Douglas Adams in *The Hitchhiker's Guide to the Galaxy* in agreeing with the view expressed through his computer, Deep Thought, that, after all, the answer to life, the universe and everything is forty-two. Or whatever number of peaks you feel moved to run up, whichever patch of water you aspire to swim through, whichever song you want to sing, scene you wish to paint or rock you dream of climbing. It is whichever next thing you want to reach for presently just a little outside your grasp. Eternal electronic humans may exist one day, but they will always be missing something, and this thing it's not e-mail, e-books or e-commerce – it's emotion. Algorithms cannot build feelings; our perfection lies in our fallibility. Emotional detachment may be considered a worthy goal by some but it surely would be hell. Not a blazing hell but an insipid boring hell where life would have no meaning. We are organically melded, not just within ourselves but with each other and with everything else. Clever little monkey that I am, I can run over Cat Bells with my hound, and, chasing each other down the rocks, we both know the meaning of life.

Fifteen
Not the Last Chapter

"Where's the last chapter?" demanded Jenn Bell.

"But I have finished."

"You're kidding. You cannot leave it out."

"No, I am finished."

Then the idea stewed for a short while, and yes, she was right: I could not leave *it* out. But I hardly know how to tell this last story; it seems so unreal to me that I can hardly believe it was actually true.

Two or three years ago, we Keswick Women had a bit of a get-together, as is customary around New Year, to see what everyone wanted to focus on in the coming year and what team events we could plan. The Billy Bland Challenge had become quite popular, and a terrible state of affairs had come to my attention. The womens' record for this team event, a relay of the Bob Graham, was held by the Sheffield-based team Dark Peak. Of course, they are a large and excellent club, and we are a small and friendly one, but, there are times when small folk need to think big. After all, the Billy Bland starts in Keswick, it finishes in

Keswick, so we simply had to bring the record to where it belonged: it was our duty. The idea began to brew. In 2016, the following year, recces were undertaken and a plan was hatched, but, by then, I was too hurt to run. The rules of the Billy Bland Challenge are that it can be done at any time in June, so we set aside some dates. For me, it was a type of torture. I was meant to be organising it and getting everyone fired up, but, in reality, I could hardly walk. I could thus hardly bear to mix with the runners, except for my close friends. But up to a few weeks beforehand, I had thought that it would still be alright and that I could organise a team without running myself. But when others started to have problems too, I dropped the baton and gave it up for lost. We needed ten strong runners, two for each leg, and they had to know the route inside out. "Let's try next year, team" was my verdict, but I was soon faced with a resound-ing reply: "No, we are doing it." I may have dropped the baton, but Katy Moore, Jo Gillyon and Cat Evans got organised and found substitutes for those who were ill or injured, and off they went. At least, I made it up to Broad Stand on Scafell to help Mandy fix the ropes on the short rock climb. Jo and Cat were on that leg, and they had joked that Mandy, with her pedigree as a difficult access expert and prowess as a window cleaner, could take a ladder up. They were quite surprised to find one secured for their use on the day! You can imagine the questions we got on the way up to Scafell on a busy Saturday morning! It was not until we were asked for the umpteenth time "Why the ladder?" by an innocent group of walkers that we thought of the perfect reply. "Oh gosh, you haven't you got one? What are you going to do?"

That day, everyone worked hard and put in some great perfor-mances, but the team was off the money, and they did not get the record. But, by then, Jo Gillyon had the bit between her teeth and was determined to organise another go in 2017.

As spring unfolded, much to everyone's amazement, I managed a couple of races on hardly any training and did not do too badly, so Jo enquired whether I would like to accompany the runners on the final leg of the Billy Bland. Three of us could set off together, and, if I could stay with them, that would be fine, but, if not, it would not matter, as the last five miles is on the road down the Newlands Valley. If I was hurting too badly, I could thus hop into a car, and it would not affect the other two. Nice of them to consider this old crock: it was a lovely gesture. I wanted to do it so much, but wanting is not enough. I went with Sam to recce the fell section running from Honister Pass over three summits, Dale Head, Hindscarth and Robinson, and the descent to Newlands. A few days later, I jogged out to the start of the road section on my own and then ran as fast as I could back to Keswick, the only real road run I had done for a couple of years. I wondered if I could put the two sections together and be okay. It was a good thing to try, and, in any case, I would not affect the team if I could not make it.

The date had been set for months, and, the week beforehand, I went sea kayaking in Scotland. On the Thursday, I was in a bunkhouse on a west-coast beach dropping off to sleep after a wild day paddling on the waves when Cat rang. "We need to know if you can really do it." Sam had a badly injured foot and, much to her disappointment, would not be able to run, so it was down to Lindsay Walker and me. I felt calm and certain.

"Yes, I can do it, but no faster than one hour fifty-five."

"That will be fine; see you on Sunday."

Sunday arrived, and the first thing Mandy and I did before even getting the morning tea was to switch on the laptop to see how Little Jenn and Katy Moore were doing on leg one. The baton was an electronic tracker which we followed on the internet all day. By 7 a.m. they had already broken the leg-one record in under three hours. Up until then, I thought Jo's schedule had been ridiculously ambitious. I should have known better. These women are strong, amazing athletes. I was by far the weakest in this team, and I had no business underestimating them.

After our breakfast, Mandy and John Byrne set out for Wasdale to go up Scafell to set the ropes on Broad Stand for Cat and Jo. I spent the next few minutes wandering around the house like a lost lamb and could not resist phoning Cat.

"Hi Jules. I'm just giving Rowan her breakfast; then it won't be long until we are off to Dunmail."

"Oh, what should I do?" I whimpered pathetically. I was meant to be resting up all day, but I literally did not know what to do with myself, and, every time I thought of a menial distraction, it only lasted a few minutes before I just had to check the progress of the tracker on the internet again. Soon, Hannah Horsburgh and Cat Spurden had a leg-two record in the bag, and Jo and Cat were off. Leg three is a long run over difficult terrain, but they stuck to the task. As they went along, I diligently checked the tracker, trying to estimate how much time it would take them to get to Wasdale. They were on Broad Stand: not long to go. Check again ten minutes later: they were still on Broad Stand. Twenty minutes, half an hour, an hour; oh my God, what has gone wrong? Lindsay arrived at my house. Messages were flying around the ether. What's happened? Eventually Lindsay got through on the phone to Little Jenn. Jenn, Carl, Katy and Lesley Malarkey (our club chairperson) had made a tour of the whole Lake District by car to be at all the changeovers after Jenn and Katy's early morning storming of leg one.

"Oh yes. They handed over well ahead of time; the tracker must have lost satellites for a while."

We breathed with relief. Sam arrived at my house, selfless as ever: even though she could not run, she came to drive Lindsay and me up to Honister. I just needed steadying Sam to be there.

It was a bright day but the sun was off the car park and it was chilly in the breeze. Like a pair of greyhounds in the traps, Lindsay and I were both trying to control ourselves. Control of energy is what this is all about, after all. If we get off by 6 p.m., we will make it; every minute beyond, and it will be touch and go. Shortly before 5.30 p.m., a shout went up: "They're coming!"

Lesley grinned as she pointed to her watch.

"Will this do you, Julie?"

Lesley gave me a hug, and Lindsay grabbed the tracker from Rachel Mellor and Trudy Beetham. They had had an astonishing run, smashing the leg-four record. Lindsay and I had loads of time, but that was not the point. Eight had gone before and given their best; how could we give any less? And every minute we took off the record would make it harder for another team to go faster.

Lindsay is faster than me uphill, but we had a plan and stuck to it. It worked like a dream, and it seemed as if we had skipped over the fells in no time. Soon, Mandy appeared on the track down to Newlands. We sped past like racehorses, and I shouted back to her in joy,

"I love you!"

"So do I," was Lindsay's hilarious addition.

Sam was at the road end with drinks and a gel. Carl and Jenn were also there, willing us on. The road is not easy, as there are a couple of tough uphill drags. We were joined by my friend Alison Scott and her daughter on bikes, and they rode ahead and watched for traffic. Mandy and Sam leap-frogged us in the car. We gathered more momentum and pushed on hard, step for step, breath for breath. We ran like one runner, perfectly in tune. While both of us were not far from the red line of total effort, we were both in control, although, in my case, only just. The final rise is just before the Swinside Inn. Lindsay turned to me beaming:

"Fancy a swift half? We've got time."

With no spare breath for words, I could only smile inside at her comic timing.

Pain came, but what of it? Soon, we were passing our back gate in Portinscale, and Mandy had our huge Jamaican flag, our souvenir from the Olympics, out, waving it all across the road. All the best teams wear yellow and green! Just another mile, and, as we crossed the Portinscale footbridge, Lindsay danced over wayward dogs and men with fishing rods to avoid a mishap. My legs were jelly, my lungs were bursting; come on, think of what the other girls did, don't let them down. Up the main street to cheers and applause, and I collapsed on the steps of the Moot Hall. I needed a couple of minutes before either standing or speaking were possible. Cat came over to me grinning: "We did fifteen twenty-two for the whole thing. Your leg was an hour forty-seven!"

The old record had been over sixteen hours. We both laughed and laughed, and then laughed some more. Even Jo's ambitious schedule, aiming for fifteen hours forty minutes, had not been ambitious enough, and we barely knew how to stop laughing.

I was the weakest runner in the team. But what mattered was that I had been in the team, and we all felt proud. And those who had run the previous year and had not been able to do so this time also made a big contribution.

So that was the unbelievable truth of what we did on the last Sunday in June 2017. Another team may go even faster in future, but Keswick Women will always own our own performance, our own day of happiness. Gifts like these are owned forever, unstealable, incorruptible.

A few weeks after the Billy, I was doing fine. Still with problems and daily pain, but these were less dominant, and I had shown myself I was still a runner. I could run two or three times a week without making anything worse. I started a new line of work which caused me less pain than the grind of general practice. I wrote an extremely modest training plan for myself. I was willing to take things steady; there were now no timetables or objectives other than slowly building up, and I was determined to give myself the best chance. I had tasted the joy of running again, and, if I played my cards right, maybe it could be back on my menu after all, even in a scaled-down form. I was deeply pleased. Times when pain gets hold of me, infests my being and makes me feel useless are still there, but much less frequently. None of us knows the future: it is all about giving ourselves the best chance. However, just as I was starting to feel pleased with myself for beginning to steer an onward course, I made a dreadful mistake.

Mandy and I had a free weekend and decided to quit the summer rain of Cumbria and climb on the gritstone edges of the Peak District. Many of the climbs there are less than twenty metres high, but they pack a punch. Gritstone climbing is an acquired taste: some love it, some hate it. Grit asks a lot in terms of coordinated whole-body movement. It is not so much about sequencing moves from one hold to the next, as there are not too many defined holds. Instead, there are rounded cracks where a clenched fist can jam, slight slabby slopes for foot placements and *elephants' arses* over which to spread one's hands like a lizard.

Grit is about balance, friction and momentum. We had done hardly any gritstone climbing in recent years, and I had lost the feel for it. After our first day, I felt humbled but consoled myself with the idea that it would come back after a few more climbs. The next day, there were fleeting moments of flow, and I began to enjoy getting the feeling of gritstone again. The Stanage Moors were vibrant purple, covered in a blanket of luxurious sweet-smelling heather. A fresh wind chilled our bones as we belayed each other at the top of each climb, looking out over the heather-honeyed moors, which rolled out to the horizon. Sun shafts over the distant hills grew hazier after each route. Rain would come soon. We gathered up the rucksack and the dog and moved along to the next buttress of strong grey grit sculptured like a fortress. Our friend Sue King popped up; she had promised to join us for a climb, as she lived nearby. Mandy and I quickly eyed a line: better get on with it while the weather lasted. Starting in haste, I wedged in a small metal nut for protection. That would keep me from hitting the ground until I got my feet on that bigger ledge and put something better in. This is how the climber's brain thinks, always looking out for ways to minimise the risk, even though you never expect to fall. I had been climbing for thirty years and hardly ever pushed myself hard enough to fall off and, even then, only when it was really safe, like on a climbing wall or bolted climb. In all those years, I had never hurt myself. Until that day. I reached over leftwards and came off the rock. As my weight came onto the rope, the protection I had hurriedly placed shaved a slither of rock from the crack edge and popped out. I hit the ground badly and knew immediately I had broken my pelvis.

"Call 999. Tell them I've broken my pelvis and will need a helicopter."

Then I screamed a bit, but it did not help, so I closed my eyes and concentrated on breathing. I wondered if I would cope. I tried to survive the next moment, to hold on, a bit like at the end of a race: just hold on, relax, breathe. There was a weird sensation of warm fluid leaking into my pelvis, and, although I had no open wound, I knew I was bleeding a lot inside. There was a pain in my chest. Everything was about the next breath, just like in a race, although no race I had done had ever hurt this bad. A kind passer-by and Mandy tried to keep me warm, covering me with their jackets, while they shivered badly. Sue went uphill to be visible and alert the rescue team to our exact location. I kept my eyes closed, and we talked about running. Of course. Something to try to divert my mind away from the agony and help to keep me calm.

As time passed, I knew I would be alright. If the internal bleeding was going to lethal, I would surely not still be conscious. After about forty minutes, Edale Mountain Rescue Team and an Air Ambulance arrived. I felt so sorry that these people had to come out for me. Although feeling guilty, I had no choice other than to surrender to their amazing and selfless kindness and excellent highly-skilled care. A whole team of people were at work together for no money just to help me. I was on the receiving end of the best of humanity. However, the care I received in hospital was not so good. After several hours of persistence on my part, I was eventually furnished with an ice pack, which provided much greater pain relief than morphine. I complained all night of being breathless and there was a grating in my chest although the medics insisted that I had nothing wrong with my chest. Having received no useful help by the next day, Mandy took me home in the van with three large pelvic fractures, nerve damage in the *undercarriage*, broken ribs and a bleed into the left lung. It was a long and tiring journey.

Nine days since the accident, and I have been for my first swim and can walk a few steps without crutches. My pelvis is still very swollen and my back and buttocks are a rainbow from deep purple to yellow. I can feel the splinting of my bones by the internal bruises and I am trusting all those clever things bodies can do to heal themselves. My thoughts inevitably turn to Kit, and I begin to feel the familiar presence of the thin insubstantial curtain which veils death from life. I too could so easily have died at the foot of a crag after a fall, and it's not so much the near-ending as the method that sobers me. In some ridiculous way, to have died at the foot of Stanage on a cold summer's Sunday, with the heather in bloom, would have been to dishonour my friend. I had not looked at the crux moves hard enough before I embarked on that climb. I thought I would just give it a go and did not have a proper plan. It would only have taken three or four minutes to consider, to look and plot and make sure that the first bit of protection was good. Mistakes can be justified only if you can learn from them. In A & E, all three of us had regrets, although Mandy's and Sue's were, in my mind, misplaced. We all knew we had to stop the regretting and *what iffing* there and then. It was done, and I am alive.

Roses are in bloom in the back garden, and the sun sets rose pink over the fells. I can make it to the back gate, and each step beyond it is a painful joy. I imagine myself on the tops of the fells – running. I imagine my fingers closing on a solid hold on a steep crag as peregrines screech. I thought I knew how to appreciate these moments, but now, in my imagination, they have a depth of colour, an exquisite vibrancy and clarity of definition which I have never known. It's a kind of natural LSD and, no, it's not the painkillers – I ditched those on day three, as they did nothing for the pain and made me vomit. The drug of gratitude is powerful. I thought I knew it, but seemingly not. I've never been quite so dosed up on appreciation, and the roses have never smelt quite so sweet. In bed with an ice pack now: it's time to try to get some rest. My nights have been fitful and sore, but, when morning comes, I will do just a little more than today, maybe have another swim. There's a club race from Fitz Park in Keswick around Latrigg tomorrow night. I amuse myself with the idea of just standing on the start line on crutches with a number on my vest just to see my team-mates' faces.

Two days later, day eleven, and I have just swum my first ever mile of front crawl, on my own, in a smooth glassy Derwentwater on a silver-clouded morning. Re-warming with porridge and hot tea, I notice an email from Wendy Dodds, who is in pot after breaking her leg. She jokes that she is the fastest crutches user in Westmorland General and wants to know when we can do the 'Frog Graham', a forty-mile fell running challenge which also involves swimming Bassenthwaite, Crummock Water, Butter-mere and Derwentwater. She seemed to think that my being a long way from running forty miles before I broke my pelvis, and being a novice swimmer, were inadequate excuses. Reliable heroes will always spur you on in the hardest moments.

It's important to say, though, that the onward journey is not about the need to achieve. Achievement is an abstract concept, and I would prefer to concern myself with real stuff. Real stuff is ten women giving their best as one team, laughing and crying, running and swearing together. Real stuff is having a real wife who always tries her best for me and real friends who, when you're broken, will do the shopping, walk the dog, share your dreams and take part in your life's script.

You may mistake the climbing of climbs, the running of races, the swimming of swims for achievements, but that is not what they are to me. To me, they are gifts received gratefully. They are the practice of living with a whole heart.

I hope I will have more chapters to write in future, but, as I come to the end of this one, I reflect on why this unremarkable bent little runner felt the need to write a book about fell running. The answer, like so many others, lies at the end of the rainbow. No story, no matter how well told, can ever make a soul completely legible. Archetypes, stereotypes, heroes, explanations and definitions will never capture one's essence. I have realised that it is not in the writing of a book but in the running of a race that I can muster the best explanation of myself. I don't mean the island-like self which began on my birthday but all the countless billions of complex forces over endless millennia, and all the ancestral adventures, that led up to the moment when a woman crosses a finish line. And when I say a finish line, I don't mean one of those inflatable edifices where you get a plastic bag full of odd stuff you didn't want and a medal. I mean a stick in a field at the bottom of a fell where I paid a couple of quid for a number out of the back of somebody's car and where there are no prizes. Where I ran my very heart out and had that feeling after the finish of not knowing whether to laugh or cry or just stand there and scoop a cup from the bucket of weak orange squash with floating grass and settling dirt and be grateful. These are the moments that come closest to anything approaching an explanation. I have discovered that they cannot be fully relived through words, but they can be acknowledged.

This book then is a sort of thanks to all the people I have ever run with and to the whole community which makes it all happen. Thanks. I'll see you when I'm mended. In the meantime, I hope you all enjoy yourselves, every lung-busting race, every run, every footstep, every last breath.

Ending
I am a Fell Runner

all I want to do is run and run into the night and into the day and feel the wind on my chest and the rain on my face and the constant movement of me through air and air through me to breathe and ask for more breath with a glutton's appetite I will eat up the ground and drink in the air I am a fellrunner and wind blows through my sedge-like hair my bones are stones my blood is rain made puddle mud my mind streams noisy bubbling undammable rushing clear crystal streams running running all I want to do is run

and then I'll go back in

the dreamtime fellrunner

will go back in

to the fell

Bibliography

Chapter 1

Csikszentmihalyi, Mihaly. Flow: *The Psychology of Optimal Experience*, Rider, 2002

Chapter 2

Askwith, Richard. *Feet in the Clouds*, Aurum Press, 2004

Buckley, Paddy, Brian Covell, Roger Smith. *42 Peaks, The Story of the Bob Graham Round,* Hayloft Publishing Ltd, Kendal, 2012

Griffin, Joe and Ivan Tyrell. *Human Givens*, Human Givens Publishing Ltd, 2004

Chapter 4

Daniels, Jack. *Daniel's Running Formula*, Human Kinetics Publishers, 2004

Whalley, Boff. *Run Wild*, Simon and Schuster UK, 2012

Chapter 8

Monbiot, George. *Feral*, Penguin Press, 2013

Chapter 9

Melzack, Patrick. Wall, Ronald. *The Challenge of Pain*, Penguin Science, 1996

Chapter 10

Nyad, Diana. *Find A Way*, Knopf Publishing, 2015

Chapter 11

Frankl, Viktor. *Man's Search For Meaning*, Rider 2004

Chapter 12

Jornet, Kilian. *Run Or Die*, Velopress, 2013

Noakes, Tim. *The Lore Of Running*, Human Kinetics Publishers, 2001

Chapter 13

Melzack, Patrick. Wall, Ronald. *The Challenge of Pain*, Penguin Science, 1996

Van Der Kolk, Bessel. *The Body Keeps the Score*, Penguin, 2015

Chapter 14

Adams, Douglas. *A Hitchhiker's Guide to the Galaxy*, William Heinemann, 1979

Deikman, Arthur. *The Observing Self*, Beacon Press, 1982

Goleman, Daniel. *Emotional Intelligence*, Bloomsbury Publishing, 1996

Hood, Bruce. *The Self Illusion*, Constable, 2013

Peters, Steve. *The Chimp Paradox*, Vermilion London, 2012

Photographs

You are invited to enjoy a series of complimentary photographs to this book which are set to music by the wonderful Cumbrian band Stooshie. Head to the Mindfell website and click on the video/audio tab. (https://www.mindfell.co.uk/videos-audio)

Many thanks to the following people for giving permission to use their photographs.

- Cat Evans
- Charlotte Pritchard
- Darian Bridge
- Dave and Eileen Woodhead
- David Hayton
- Ed Gamble
- Edale Mountain Rescue Team
- Geoff Ayers
- John Nicoll
- Mandy Glanvill
- Peter Crosby

- Reinier Schrader
- Sarah Bailey
- Stephen Wilson
- Sue King

Acknowledgements

It is a long journey between starting to write and ending up with a book. As in all my endeavours in life, without the help of others I would not have made it.

I would like to say thank you to all my friends, team-mates and competitors, many of whom are mentioned in the book, with many others not named but still appreciated. May I play my part in your scripts as well as you have played yours in mine.

A special thanks to Cathy Woodhead of Delfryn Publications, who, with a dedicated effort and unwavering enthusiasm, turned the manuscript into the original book.

I am very grateful to those who have given permission for the publication of the accompanying photographs which you can view on my website www.mindfell.co.uk under the video and audio tab.

Huge thanks to Vincent Booth for his lovely cover painting.

And thanks to Mandy for nothing less than everything.

About the Author

Julie Carter grew up in Sunderland and lives near Keswick in Cumbria, UK. She started her working life as a researcher in genetics before teaching science and outdoor education then becoming a medical doctor. After a couple of decades working in emergency care and general practice, she began to look more broadly for different ways of promoting health and alleviating distress. This led her to train in Human Givens which is an evidence-based practical approach to health based on getting our needs met in balance, without exploiting others.

Julie is a runner, a climber and an adventurer. Her experiences in all aspects of her life are the inspiration for her writing which crosses the genres of creative non- fiction and poetry. Her second book, 'Is It Serious?', is a collection of short works on the subjects of family, love, science, medicine and wild things. Julie enjoys forming collaborations, making connections and speaking at events and festivals. She has worked with the filmmaker Jessie Leong and their film 'I Am A Fellrunner' has won laurels at nine film festivals worldwide. The film is available free on YouTube and also on the Mindfell website where you can find a further selection of Julie's work including film and audio as well as the all the back issues of her popular Mindfell Monthly Blog.

Julie's third book, 'Makin a Mackem: The journey of running into my skin' will be published in the autumn of 2023. 'Makin a Mackem' is the story of Julie's three day run across the north of England, from Keswick to Gateshead, to honour a significant ancestor. It is an exploration of inheritance weaving in evolutionary biology, history and psychology into a real-life adventure.

Following the publication of her experimental essay 'The Scafells - A Place of Highest Honour' in Saraband's 'North Country' Anthology in 2022 Julie is now is working on a book of lyric essays on themes around how we find safety in a threatening world. Supported by Arts Council England Julie is also continuing to work on her theatre show 'The Dreamtime Fellrunner' with a plan to tour the show in 2024.

Julie is always pleased to have creative conversations and receive comment on her work. Contact details are on the Mindfell website: www.mindfell.co.uk

Printed in Dunstable, United Kingdom